FORGED IN BATTLE

Forged in Battle

Jan Breytenbach

PROTEA BOOK HOUSE
PRETORIA
2014

First edition, first impression in 1986 by Saayman & Weber (Pty) Ltd
Second edition, first impression in 2014 by Protea Book House

PO Box 35110, Menlo Park, 0102
1067 Burnett Street, Hatfield, Pretoria
8 Minni Street, Clydesdale, Pretoria.
protea@intekom.co.za
www.proteaboekhuis.co.za

Editor: Danél Hanekom
Proofreader: Caren van Houwelingen
Cover design by Hanli Deysel
Cover photographs by Al J. Venter
Photographs inside book by Cloete Breytenbach
Set in 10.35 on 13.15 pt ZapfCalligr BT by Ada Radford
Printed and bound by Creda

© 1986, 2014 Jan Breytenbach
ISBN: 978-1-4853-0044-1 (printed book)
ISBN: 978-1-4853-0045-8 (e-book)

No part of this book may be reproduced or transmitted in any form
or by any electronic or mechanical means, including photocopying
and recording or by any other information storage or retrieval system,
without written permission from the publisher.

Foreword

The author has written about a period in our military history. He starts at one point and works his way systematically through a series of events to arrive at another point. He succeeds masterfully in refraining from a cold and impersonal discussion of this segment of history. With material like this, an author can easily fall into the trap of "and then this happened, and then that happened". The birth and growth of 32 Battalion is reported clearly and factually without it ever reading like a history textbook.

The excellent way in which the author uses language lends finesse to the book, yet every now and then Jan Breytenbach does surface and it is as if one is sitting under a camel-thorn tree listening to interesting stories told by this extraordinary and sometimes controversial man. His humour and distinctive style often gives one an insight into the extremely human soul of the Jan Breytenbach masked behind the rough and almost frightening exterior of the hardened soldier.

In writing this foreword I consulted my friend and brother officer, Colonel Delville Linford, who was very much a part of the whole story. He said:

"It is difficult to prevent your objectivity from being coloured either by your own experience of the situation or by a measure of hero worship for the author, especially if one was intensely involved in the events and knows the author personally.

"Jan has an eye for detail and he must have an excellent memory. I have never seen him taking notes and am not aware of him keeping a diary at all, but the precise detail with which he describes the circumstances, environment and incidents is almost unbelievable. This becomes even more stunning if one bears in mind that many of these incidents took place under severe pressure, leaving little time for taking down notes for a book. When one reads the book, however, it is amazing how vividly one is able to remember the actual scenes and events."

Jan Breytenbach is almost poignantly just in the handling of the characters in his book. Those who have made an impression on him receive the necessary praise without it ever being "soppy", while those unfortunate enough to find themselves on the wrong side of him are hammered, but still in such a way that the reader is able to digest it and the unfortunate individual concerned cannot sue him for libel. He does not only evaluate others, but he also has the ability to analyse his own actions to even judge them almost objectively.

It goes without saying that the birth of a unit such as 32 Battalion has to be accompanied by the inevitable birth pangs. In Breytenbach's book the wretchedness, accompanying these pains, is often visible, but always sketched with a smile through the tears, and the reader is never confronted with the absolutely sordid.

To create an effective war machine out of an untrained, undisciplined group of men is no mean feat. One is always aware of the pleasure he takes in his work and of the fact that he is very proud of the result he has produced. This he does simply, and without being ostentatious. One never gets the impression of "I did this and I did that", but still clearly notes what he has achieved. This is emphasised best perhaps by the often modest way in which he tells his story.

To conclude, here is Delville again: "I am proud to have had the opportunity to share a part of my life with Jan Breytenbach and to have been influenced by his professionalism. He is a man of stature who has written a part of our country's history. He built a monument on which the South African Defence Force and the past, present, and future members of 32 Battalion can be justly proud."

General J.J. Geldenhuys, SSA, SD, SM
(Former Chief of the South African Defence Force)

Contents

Introduction   9
 1. Training Mission   11
 2. Shaping the Unit   20
 3. Is UNITA the Enemy?   30
 4. Off to War   37
 5. First Clash – UNITA   44
 6. Pereira de Eça   55
 7. Attack on Sá da Bandeira   65
 8. Moçâmedes   82
 9. Joining up with Frank   93
10. Catengue   97
11. Courage and Cowardice   117
12. Cubale   124
13. Benguela   135
14. Marking Time   146
15. Novo Redondo   158
16. Cela   181
Epilogue   204
List of Names   207

Introduction

This is the story of the birth of 32 Battalion during the Savannah campaign in Angola. The battalion, first known as Bravo Group, was formed from the ill-disciplined and badly trained remnants of the Chipenda faction of FNLA. The FNLA forces had been badly mauled when the MPLA forcibly ousted them and their UNITA allies from the central government in Luanda.

The formation and training of Bravo Group was undertaken in a great hurry, so much so that a very flawed unit finally crossed the Angolan frontier to do battle with the MPLA and their Cuban allies. Fortunately for us our introduction into the frenzy and chaos of battle was very gradual. This gave me the opportunity to complete the forging of a very formidable instrument under the most realistic, if somewhat trying, conditions. I cannot think of a better way to train troops than under fire, but then the enemy must also "play ball". Inadvertently they did. When my troops were finally severely tested under tremendous fire from both MPLA and Cuban forces, they carried the day, often with elán but always with their tails right up.

This is the story about a battalion – its officers, NCOs and troops and not its commander. It was an honour to command these men in battle. To them, white and black, South African or Angolan, this book is dedicated. It was a rare joy to have experienced their complete loyalty and trust, to have had the opportunity to personally lead them in battle and to know that they would be there at all times, fighting shoulder to shoulder with a commander from the "racist" south who could not even speak their language.

It was with great satisfaction that I could experience with them their progress from confused and bungling amateurs to hard-bitten and tough professionals, generally acknowledged as the best fighting troops in the South African Army.

ONE
Training Mission

Seventy-five kilometres north-east of Rundu, capital of the Kavango homeland, lies a small former Portuguese marine base called M'pupa. It lies on the west bank of the Cuito River, a short distance from the M'pupa Falls. The base marks the downstream end of the navigable stretch of river between it and another former Portuguese marine base, Vila Nova D'Armada, which is about three days' travel upstream by gunboat.

Portuguese marines patrolled this stretch of water during the guerrilla war that lasted from 1961 until the beginning of 1975 when the Portuguese metropolitan government was brought to its knees by their own communist-infiltrated armed forces.

They patrolled against UNITA and MPLA guerrillas who crossed the Cuito in gangs from the uninhabited east bank to the populated west bank, to either intimidate the population in order to gain support, MPLA fashion, or to spread their message by indoctrination – a more acceptable way, which was how Dr Jonas Savimbi elected to spread the UNITA gospel.

There were, of course, numerous armed clashes between MPLA and UNITA with the Portuguese administration surreptitiously supporting UNITA. They rarely if ever launched operations against UNITA and there are indications that they even supplied them with arms and ammunition in certain parts of south and eastern Angola.

During the end of 1974 and the beginning of 1975, however, the MPLA in southern Angola began, under the leadership of Daniel Chipenda, the MPLA military commander, to have some doubts about the MPLA cause. A leadership struggle had developed between Chipenda and Agostinho Neto, the "president" of MPLA, which eventually culminated in most of the MPLA in the south and east breaking away and throwing in their lot with FNLA. FNLA was commanded by Holden Roberto from the safety of Zaire. Chipenda's ex-MPLA, now FNLA, therefore operated from the same power base in the south of Angola, which they established when they were still in competition with Savimbi's UNITA. There was certainly no love lost between the two movements, even though they were now fighting MPLA as a common enemy.

The sudden Portuguese abdication quite naturally brought about a power struggle between the three liberation movements, MPLA, FNLA and UNITA. Each movement was intent on gaining as much ground as possible before 11 November 1975, which was the date the Portuguese would hand over the country to either a coalition or to the strongest of the three.

With this in mind, Jonas Savimbi and Holden Roberto teamed up against MPLA which, after Chipenda's defection with most of the MPLA army (commonly known as the FAPLA) was in a weak position militarily.

With the assistance of the communist-infiltrated Portuguese armed forces, however, the help of Cuba was obtained to re-structure, re-equip and retrain FAPLA. In a short space of time a large and well-equipped FAPLA army was deployed through all of central Angola, most of southern Angola and parts of the east and the north. They were backed up by the first contingents from the Cuban Army, which started arriving in Angola towards the middle of 1975.

The situation in southern Angola became quite chaotic with towns changing hands frequently between any of the three movements. It became difficult for the South Africans, on the southern banks of the Okavango and Cunene rivers to determine which troops from which movement they were facing across the border, whether they were actively hostile or not, or whether they were perhaps SWAPO supporters, passively or otherwise. Most were wearing Portuguese camouflage and many, from all three movements, carried not only AK-74s, but also G3 rifles, the standard rifle issued to the Portuguese Army.

To add to the confusion, hundreds of "flechas" – former

black or Bushmen Portuguese soldiers – were drifting aimlessly across the countryside trying to find a home with one of the three movements. Most of them ended up in Chipenda's FNLA, mainly because this particular faction had developed into a fairly slick gangster mob which preyed on banks, businesses and quite often the unfortunate white Portuguese settlers. Money and loot were therefore to be had with FNLA, whereas UNITA only offered a "highfalutin" cause and MPLA (FAPLA) the highly undesirable and harsh discipline of their Cuban mentors and taskmasters.

On the exceedingly hot and dry August afternoon as I flew towards M'pupa, with the mission to make contact with FNLA, I was not at all sure whether M'pupa would still be in the hands of Chipenda's men. The latest information, several weeks old, indicated that FNLA was the most recent occupant, but it had changed hands several times during the past year. It was with a feeling of trepidation that we approached the base, shimmering in the dry afternoon heat, at the eastern end of a dusty airstrip hacked out of the bush by the former Portuguese garrison.

The pilot was Jules, expertly in charge of the two-motored Aztec. His intention was to fly over the base at some height so that we could have a look at the flag, FNLA colours being red, white and yellow. Unfortunately, there was not enough breeze to even stir the limp rag hanging from a pole at the entrance to the base. We could make out the red but were not too sure about any yellow or white.

The UNITA flag was red and green and it could therefore also easily be a UNITA garrison occupying the base. This would be bad news for us because at the time, a lot of SWAPO (the terrorist organisation operating in South West Africa against the South African forces) were to be found in UNITA ranks. White throats would surely be cut, especially if we arrived unannounced.

Then, of course, there was the red and black banner of MPLA. They would consider it a great privilege to rid Africa of four white capitalists, three of whom belonged to hated racists from the south.

Jules decided to land short from west to east and to keep the motors running after landing.

The three of us, Coen, a staff officer from the sector headquarters, Pelissa, an Italian farming in Angola and on friendly terms with Chipenda, and myself would approach the base very carefully on foot to determine, from a distance, which organisation was in occupation. In the event of a shootout, or if the wrong people were *in situ*, we would rush back to Jules and his Aztec and hope for a quick takeoff before collecting too many holes in either body or plane.

As Jules crossed the western threshold of the runway, there was a stirring of some troops on the far side. He put the Aztec down in a cloud of dust and by use of brakes came to a halt less than halfway down the strip. Although a bush strip, the Portuguese had built it long enough to take their lumbering Noratlas transport aircraft.

Three of us scrambled out into the blast furnace heat while Jules ensconced himself on one wing with an Uzi to cover our afternoon stroll towards the base. The engines were still running.

With false bravado Coen and I went right and left respectively, our rifles at the ready and keeping as much cover as possible between us and the base, while Pelissa, as huge as a tank, strode majestically down the centre of the runway armed with his walking stick, a ten-gallon hat squarely settled on his head. He evidently was completely unafraid, or completely convinced that the troops approaching us from the eastern end were FNLA and not potential enemy.

These troops had split into two sections, each about eight strong, on each side of the runway and with a caution that matched our own, they approached the Aztec and the three advancing white men.

At a distance they all seemed to be armed and the way they were carrying their weapons, at the ready, and darting from cover to cover did not exactly fill me with a feeling of confidence and joy that we would be meeting with an enthusiastic bunch of our future comrades in arms.

In fact, I was more than apprehensive. I felt the heavy cold stone of fear settling in the pit of my stomach and a distinct inclination to lag behind the other two. A glance over my shoulder at Jules squatting on the wing of the Aztec with the Uzi in his hands did not reassure me either.

Most pilots I knew were pretty useless with small arms, although they may be damn good with a rocket-slung Mirage fighter bomber. I wondered whether Jules had the safety catch off or whether he had even remembered to put in a fully-loaded magazine.

Gradually the approaching blacks, mostly in Portuguese type camouflage, leapfrogged closer and closer.

Pelissa undisturbedly strode along the hot dusty runway, swinging his cane. Coen and I moved forward in unison, reluctantly on my part. How Coen felt I had no idea.

Suddenly a figure, better dressed than the others, wearing a black beret and typical calf-length Russian army boots, disengaged himself from the one section and strode purposefully towards Pelissa.

Russian boots. Not a hopeful sign at all, but it did not seem to disturb Pelissa. In fact, he increased his pace until the two were at embracing distance from each other.

"Pelissa!"

"Domingos!"

There was a lot of hugging and backslapping in the centre of the runway, streams of Portuguese and the audible sighs of relief as Coen and I put on our safety catches and slung our rifles.

The two sections gathered with Pelissa and Domingos shaking hands and spouting away in Portuguese.

Coen and I were introduced. Jules climbed back into the Aztec and taxied it down to the eastern end. We all walked to the base to meet the rest of the FNLA garrison.

The base was in a filthy state. The approaches were through a several-hundred-metre-wide minefield of human excrement through which one had to step very gingerly indeed in order not to fall foul of these anti-personnel devices. Millions of flies swarmed everywhere and the stench was all-pervading. Papers, old empty beer bottles, plastic containers and all sorts of rubbish were littered everywhere in the camp itself.

The only reasonably clean place was the headquarters building with two or three offices, each with metal desks and some rickety chairs. There was even a typewriter on which a troop was banging away, probably at some high-sounding order of the day issued in the name of Chipenda and exhorting FNLA to fight until the bitter end.

The barracks were reasonable constructions, assembled by the marines as prefabs from metal panels bolted together. They were, however, in a filthy state with virtually every windowpane and door broken.

In the south-west corner there was a pretty thatched and whitewashed little chapel, not used for its original role, but rather as a storeroom for the few bits of equipment the garrison had at their disposal. Priests and religion had departed this benighted land long ago.

Domingos was the commander of the 300 FNLA present in the base. More FNLA were coming in from the north and the west almost daily as they were seeking to escape from FAPLA and also from UNITA.

Pelissa wasted no time in telling Domingos that their problems were over, that I had come to take command of all FNLA and to train them and that I would lead them in a victorious campaign to wrest Angola from MPLA's grip.

All this was in Portuguese, of course, and I could not understand a word. Completely unaware of the gist of Pelissa's disclosures to Domingos, I therefore smiled inanely from time to time and nodded my head in apparent agreement.

Domingos was delighted. He put his arm around my shoulder and clapped me on the back, all the while spouting in Portuguese.

I did likewise, clapping him on his back and spouting away in English, shaking hands and generally feeling very happy with the fact that Domingos was so well disposed towards me and that contact with FNLA had been effected with so much friendliness all round.

"There will now be a parade," said Pelissa in his broken English, "and you must attend the parade."

Well, I thought, a turnout by the troops for me, a South African officer to pay their respects, would not be out of place. It would, in fact, be an honour.

There was a lot of shouting and from the shade of the stinking barrack buildings, there rose very reluctantly a few hundred blacks from the prone siesta position. After much stretching and yawning, they shambled off to the hot, dusty, paper-strewn parade ground.

The gallant, intrepid FNLA forces of Chipenda were forming up in crooked lines with their so-called "commandantes", about 40 of them, off to one flank.

When all was ready I was invited to get on Parade by Domingos. We strolled off to take up a position opposite the main body. Pelissa fell in behind my right shoulder from where he could brief me about what was going on and to act as my prompter in the right places.

Domingos called the parade to attention and to present arms. He saluted, I saluted, the troops came to the Portuguese stand-easy position and Domingos started to harangue his men in Portuguese. It was interspersed with a lot of "FNLA Oyezs", which I gathered was the FNLA battle cry. Every now and again I caught the mention of Chipenda's name, once or twice Holden Roberto's name and towards the end my name began to feature more.

I was beginning to get a distinctly uneasy feeling that the situation was getting away from me. Suddenly the speech stopped, the troops were called to attention, presented arms and Domingos threw a long salute. "You are now in command of Chipenda's FNLA in southern Angola". This from Pelissa behind my right shoulder.

I gulped. I had come to make contact and ended up with an army. What would I tell the Brigadier?

I returned the salute. There followed a lot of "Viva Carpenters" and "FNLA Oyezs" while I looked at my "army", all 300 of them.

They were, without a doubt, the scruffiest, most underfed, worst armed and most unwarlike body of troops I had ever seen in my life.

On my left stood the reasonably well-fed and clad "commandantes", all armed with brand-new 9 mm, FN pistols which they got from heaven knows where. Pistols are, of course, perfectly useless in a high-intensity war, except for killing oneself when things get tough and with the outlook for one's future wellbeing distinctly gloomy.

In front of me stood the troops, with the better-clad and armed group that met us on the runway, to my right. They had about twenty or so rifles of various makes among them, G3s, AK-47s and a few FN rifles.

The further to the left that my eyes went, the more desperate the future of my newly acquired FNLA army appeared.

Few troops had reasonable footwear. Those who had footwear often wore the ridiculous high-platformed and most uncomfortable shoes favoured by layabouts in the cities of Angola. Some wore yellow, red or bright green trousers with sharply contrasting, brightly coloured shirts. Many wore baseball caps and there were quite a number staring at me with sunglasses of darkest tint and often of the reflecting variety, hiding their eyes from my scrutiny.

Many were barefoot with ulcerating sores caused by malnutrition on their feet and legs. All had the grey look of hunger about them. In fact, through Pelissa I was given to understand that they were down to their last two bags of mealie meal.

Among them, in the rear rank, I spotted a dozen or so Bushmen, impassively staring to their front, showing no interest in the proceedings whatsoever. They were, obviously, former Portuguese "flechas" who had joined the enemy they had once hunted very successfully. There was no other way for them or their families to stay alive. The FNLA cause held no attraction for them whatsoever.

What I saw brought to mind the famous incident when Wellington inspected and addressed his troops before Waterloo. "You may not frighten the enemy, but by God, you frighten me!" he said as he surveyed his several thousand men, very much better equipped, trained and disciplined than my half-starved, ill-equipped, undisciplined, untrained and untried mob of 300, with which, according to promises made by Pelissa, I was on the point of conquering all of Angola.

After the "march past" – more of a shuffle past – I left the parade ground and was promptly congratulated by Jules with my new-found status and appointment. He was highly amused, of course, and so was Coen.

Only Pelissa was unperturbed as he sincerely extended his congratulations with the rider that he had informed the garrison that I would feed, clothe and arm them as the highest priority and that they had to send the word around to all FNLA in southern Angola to gather at M'pupa where I would ring in a new dawn of FNLA conquest and power.

We took off from M'pupa, with Domingos and the commandantes waving cheerfully goodbye to their new commander, no doubt visualising bags of mealie meal, tons of meat, beautiful camouflage uniforms and brand-new rifles rolling up in the morning from the direction of Rundu.

I sat grimly next to Jules pondering how I would go about equipping, training and disciplining a mob of virtual gangsters. Worst of all, how would I break the news that I was now a FNLA commander to the Brigadier and how would I obtain the goods from him to keep Pelissa's promises?

Pelissa was smiling from ear to ear. FNLA, and Pelissa, were back in business, especially Pelissa who, incidentally, owned five farms in Angola, four of which he had lost to MPLA. He had every intention of getting his farms back, and I was going to help him.

TWO
Shaping the Unit

The Brigadier was an elderly gentleman, a successful farmer from the Western Transvaal, who could be as stubborn as a thorn tree. I suppose one must be stubborn to farm in the uncertain conditions of these parts.

Because he was a reserve officer, he was also a man who did not have his mind cluttered with all the bureaucratic nonsense which seems to clutter the minds of most professional officers. He could quickly get down to the kernel of a problem, discarding all the sideshows along the way as unnecessary and time-consuming.

The Brigadier could therefore give a decision quickly. He could also be difficult, especially if one acted outside his concept of the operation. Unfortunately, it was not always clear in which direction he was going, not so much because of his lack of communication, but mainly because whatever was to happen in Angola was considered highly classified.

Apart from being told to contact FNLA and to arrange for their training, I had no idea what the future was holding for us, FNLA, UNITA and Angola in general. I assumed that we would give training and military aid only to FNLA to enable them to claim a stake of the country, which had to be as large as possible, before 11 November 1975.

Aid to UNITA, according to my reckoning, was out because they supported SWAPO and SWAPO was our own personal enemy who killed South African troops and the civilians on our side of the border. UNITA was therefore an enemy that had to be dealt with. The best organisation to deal with them would probably be FNLA. So I thought.

I was to discover later that the Brigadier and I did not see eye to eye on this matter.

Meanwhile the report back, unexpectedly, went smoothly. Apparently I operated within the Brigadier's major plan and he thought it was quite a joke to have me commanding a black FNLA unit of uncertain potential after having commanded a crack specialist unit previously.

Arms and equipment would be forthcoming, including suitable fatigues. The biggest priority, food for the starving troops, would be arranged right away.

Some men from my old unit had already reported to assist me in the training task.

I quickly got hold of Jack, a paratrooper captain, and promptly passed the buck. He had to arrange for the drawing of rations, getting hold of some vehicles, transporting the food and the vehicles across the river at night at some remote point where nobody could see what we were about and finally he had to deliver it all to M'pupa before the troops starved to death.

The Okavango River is a big river and even in August, just before the rainy season, it holds enough water to make it unfordable. It is also a very winding river, looping about in a very wide flood plain with many side channels, horseshoe lagoons and swampy areas. Crossing such a river is therefore quite a challenge if no crossing site exists.

Jack quite wisely and fortunately obtained the use of some ten-ton trucks on the Angolan side. We had to supply the diesel. However, an engineer effort was still needed, with assault craft to deliver the food and some arms and ammunition on the north bank of the river.

This was successfully done and the trucks were loaded. Then the fun and games started, moving the heavily loaded lorries across the flood plains to firm ground and the road to Dirico.

It was around midday the next day that a very muddy Jack reported to me in Rundu. All his vehicles were firmly stuck in the mud on a wide open plain with curious civilian onlookers gathering around to marvel at the tons of mealie meal, tinned meat and so on that was obviously being transported to some destination in Angola. It was hoped that they were less curious about the weapons and ammunition which were hidden underneath the rations.

They had never seen so much food in their lives, coming, as they did, from a very impoverished part of Angola and speculation, probably tinged with some hope, was therefore rife.

Opposite Rundu there used to be a small town on the Angolan side, called Calais. This town is now almost razed to the ground. Quite a strong FNLA contingent lived there, consisting of politicians, some troops and all sorts of shady characters who made their living by smuggling commodities from the Kavango into Angola. There was also a small UNITA presence, but they were forced to keep a very low profile. In fact, some of the UNITAs used to spend time on a fairly regular basis in the local FNLA jail. UNITA members also disappeared from time to time, especially after upheavals involving supporters of the two organisations.

Jack was sent to the FNLA political leader of the area (who also controlled the black market) to provide a tractor to pull out the trucks. This he agreed to do if we would supply him with some extra drums of diesel for his Land Rover and other possibly more shady purposes.

The rest of the day Jack and his men dug and pulled the trucks out of the mud and they then set course for Dirico, at the point where the Cuito and the Okavango rivers meet, before turning north for M'pupa along the west bank of the Cuito. The going was better along the riverbanks than along the existing short cut through the bush from Calais to M'pupa, this being a deeply rutted sand track.

I gathered the rest of my men two days later. We took the short cut with my Toyota and a Unimog, carrying all our personal equipment. Towards the afternoon we arrived at our destination to be met by a still starving mob of troops, which had now increased to something like 500 men. Jack and the food trucks were nowhere in sight.

Domingos was none too happy at this state of affairs. The last of the mealie meal was eaten two days previously and he was convinced that some of the men were on the point of dying of hunger. The troops were lying about listlessly in the shade, which did look rather ominous but may also have been deliberately and dramatically staged.

Jack had to be found quickly and the only means available was the Unimog.

About 15 kilometres south, towards Dirico, the first truck was found, firmly stuck in the sand. With the help of the Unimog, it was extracted from its sandy grip and later on towards sundown the first rations to reach M'pupa in weeks were driven through the main gate. It was almost a small-scale repetition of the famous Malta convoy when one oil tanker made Grand Harbour, the rest having been sunk along the way, just in time to beat off the Germans. In this case it was, of course, hunger that was kept at bay and judging by the reaction of the troops, they were certainly trying to convey that impression in a dramatic manner.

In the cool of the evening the truck was offloaded enthusiastically and off to the cookhouse went the first bags of mealie meal and some tinned meat. Soon they were filling their empty bellies with vast helpings of porridge and bully beef.

It was not long before eating became of secondary importance. As the troops got filled up with the hastily prepared "scoll", so the noise level increased until it appeared, to me anyway, that all 500 troops were conversing at the top of their voices, almost shouting, each one endeavouring to make himself heard above the din. This noise level, especially in the early mornings when they woke up, was to give me near fits of hysteria in the months ahead.

We moved off to the falls and to Pelissa's old house on the riverbank to get away from the din and also the flies and the stench pervading the main camp.

Over the next 24 hours Jack brought in the rest of the trucks. By this time the first load from the first truck had virtually been consumed so that reinforcements were welcome.

We now started to organise the troops into companies, platoons and sections. There were enough troops to form two rifle companies, each with three rifle platoons and a support company with a mortar platoon, machine-gun platoon and an anti-tank platoon.

Jack commanded B Company with three young South African corporals as platoon leaders. Connie, a lieutenant, commanded A Company with three former Portuguese soldiers as platoon leaders. "Fingers", a sergeant, commanded the machine-gun platoon and "Oupa", another sergeant, commanded the mortar platoon. I was still looking for an anti-tank platoon leader.

There were no headquarters staff as such because there were none available. I had only one radio operator, a South African Portuguese, and had appointed one of the former FNLA commandantes as my intelligence officer.

This intelligence officer was an old hand at guerrilla war. He had been trained in Russia and North Korea and had been in the bush virtually nonstop since 1961 or thereabouts. Small wonder the old guy fancied himself as a staff officer as he was getting rather tired of fighting. Judging from the impeccable clean lines of his rather worn AK-47, he must have been quite a formidable fighter in his day.

His idea of compiling and evaluating intelligence was to go off into the bush himself to gather the necessary information, probably from the local population. He would thus disappear for days on end to reappear with some rather hair-raising stories about a SWAPO presence virtually all around us.

It took me some time to tumble to the fact that FNLA made no distinction between SWAPO and UNITA. They were also clever enough to play the South Africans off against UNITA by emphasising the SWAPO factor.

I left my old "spy", ex-bushfighter, to his own devices to build up a reasonable intelligence picture of the whole area and particularly along the Okavango river line. I felt that the river line had to be secured to assure our logistics, and that we must be able to pinpoint and eradicate any potential armed interference with our supply lines before it could materialise.

I was already getting trouble from the region of Cuangar where FNLA troops, on their way to M'pupa, had been waylaid, beaten up and sometimes killed. Cuangar, by all accounts, was a SWAPO nest on the Okavango River, about 150 kilometres upstream from Rundu and therefore also a real threat to SWA.

Another SWAPO nest, according to "spy", was at Mucusso, also on the Okavango River, but about 150 kilometres downstream from Rundu.

I was already, in my own mind, tentatively beginning to plan operations along the river to clear my back door as a first stage to further operations that may be forthcoming, depending on the Brigadier's plans.

Further to the west, opposite Ovambo in the Ruacana area, he had launched a splendid little operation inside Angola during which quite a number of UNITA and presumably SWAPO bit the dust. It was therefore clear to me who the enemy was as far as South Africa was concerned.

My biggest priority, however, remained training. I was given two weeks in which to train my battalion. Luckily this ridiculously short period was extended later by several weeks. However, it forced me to concentrate my training on only a few very important aspects and to cut out not only frills but also the training of the troops in some rather desirable accomplishments.

Our efforts went into weapon training and the attack only, hoping that we would later on get time to train the troops in the other phases of war and in the real nitty-gritty of minor and guerrilla tactics, not to mention the training of specialists such as signallers, assault pioneers, drivers and so on.

In spite of a very much shortened syllabus, training was still an immense headache. The troops knew nothing, were unfit and not yet properly equipped with uniforms and weapons. Many of the commandantes refused to undergo training with the troops because, according to them, they knew everything. Many of them left after being divested of their weapons and, in some cases, their Land Rovers. We needed both weapons and vehicles badly and all equipment therefore was the common property of Chipenda's army, not of individual commandantes who were none too happy with losing their status and accompanying perks.

The mortar platoon was equipped with old three-inch mortars, well worn in the yokes, with the result that a shot could go virtually anywhere, including, at times, the target. Oupa did a splendid job, however, in training 12 mortar crews in spite of the language difficulties. He had a beautiful sense of humour and would regale us nightly on his experiences of the day with his somewhat "dim" and awkward mortar crews. But he never gave up. Of course some of the drills had to be modified including a drill, which he brought in, whereby the laying of each mortar was checked before mortars could fire for effect. Oupa therefore became a very fit young man running around among 12 mortar tubes to check up on each and every one of them constantly while firing was in progress. Failing such checks the results could, of course, be disastrous, not for the enemy, but for us keeping in mind the general worn-out state of the weapons and the capability of the crew.

"Fingers" reluctantly took charge of the Vickers machine guns. There are few infantrymen who have a love for this obsolete weapon. The gun is extremely heavy and cumbersome, has far too many stoppages and generally looked old-fashioned, a relic from the trenches of the First World War. We had 12 weapons formed into one platoon.

Soon Fingers and my feelings for the weapon began to grow to acceptance and finally, towards the end of the campaign, to downright enthusiastic respect for its fire-power and capabilities.

All infantrymen regard the Vickers as primarily a defensive weapon, but in our scheme of things there was not much scope for a defensive weapon. We therefore improvised our tactics and drills to use the machine gun in a more aggressive role, firstly by mounting them on Land Rovers, confiscated from the commandantes, and secondly by practising quick deployment to the flanks from which targets could be nicely engaged, while the infantry attacked on foot. With 12 Vickers machine guns stuttering away, their fire converging on the target, it was quite an impressive sight to see tracers and dust engulfing the hated enemy. Our troops were very impressed and clearly felt that we could take on all comers.

Finally our brand-new FN rifles and fatigue uniforms arrived. The troops were in seventh heaven with all the new equipment, particularly the uniforms and boots. They began to look like soldiers at least, although they still had a long way to go to become operational troops.

The mortar and machine-gun crews were less happy because they were stuck with Second World War Sten guns as their personal weapons.

A Sten looks crude, is in fact crudely welded together and is more dangerous to the uninitiated than to the enemy. It has the nasty habit of discharging a round when the butt end is slammed on the ground or any hard surface. Many an inexperienced troop came to grief because of this dangerous characteristic.

Training started every day with a cross-country run, followed by weapon training until about eleven o'clock, thereafter some section, platoon and company drills, a siesta in the heat of the day from 12 till three p.m. It was now early September and extremely hot. Further drills until about six p.m., an evening meal and then, more often than not, some night training.

It was a heavy day for all, including the troops, but as their energy and stamina began to build up from the consumption of vast quantities of good food and from training, so their discipline began to get somewhat out of hand.

The remaining commandantes were incapable or unwilling to maintain discipline. I was reluctant to use my own men to mete out punishment because the consequences could be unpredictable. The whole lot could turn against us or could decide to take the gap back into the bush.

The troops had the habit of going down to the river during siesta time to wash, catch fish or just to lie around. In spite of numerous inspections for loose ammunition, they would always manage to squirrel some away somewhere. Every afternoon was therefore punctuated with the discharging of rifles. Whether they were shooting at birds, fish or each other I could never really ascertain.

Now there is nothing that upsets an instructor more than the uncontrolled discharge of weapons. I therefore warned them that they had to stop firing their weapons indiscriminately because we were a very nervous bunch of instructors. So nervous, in fact, that we were liable to assume that we were under attack by an enemy. This did not help.

I therefore had a machine gun mounted at our little camp from where we could nicely overlook the river area and M'pupa. Fire would be returned in future.

And so it happened. The very next day some indiscriminate shooting went on down at the river. Fingers opened up with a long burst from his Vickers, the tracers streaking over the heads of the troops washing or swimming. Within seconds the river cleared and there was a deathly hush for the rest of the afternoon, not even raised voices could be heard from the main base itself.

For two or three days this seemed to work, but then the shooting started up again. Once more I told them that we would assume that we were under attack but that, next time, there would be an assault on foot into the area the shots were coming from.

It fell on deaf ears until one afternoon when we were returning to our camp in the Unimog. Suddenly there was a lot of shooting to our right front, bullets flying all over the place. "Right, let's dismount and attack them. Keep your fire low."

There were eight of us and we spread out in extended line while moving into the thick bush in the direction of the shooting.

At the right moment we suddenly opened fire, this time not bothering to raise the fire above their heads. With war whoops, shouting and much shooting we closed in on the "enemy". Ahead we could hear branches breaking as they took off in panic. All shooting had ceased abruptly.

We swept through the area and found nothing, to my relief, because I was fully expecting a few bodies to be lying around. Maybe our own shooting also needed some sharpening up.

This was the last time we had to suffer the indiscriminate discharging of weapons. It was also good to see the sudden alacrity in carrying out orders and the general improvement in discipline. Whinging and whining stopped completely, except from some of the commandantes. It was also at this stage that the troops' loyalty began to shift from the old commandantes to the new commandantes.

They had discovered that we evidently meant business, that we were serious in knocking an operational battalion together, fit to fight wherever it may be required.

THREE
Is UNITA the Enemy?

There appeared on the scene a new commandante, evidently senior to Domingos in the FNLA hierarchy. He was known as Double O, or Oginga Odinga, obviously a war name he adopted as a sign of admiration for the Kenyan radical politician of that name. This fact did not auger well for the future as we shall see later.

Double O, however, was more effective than Domingos in that he took firm control of the troops in camp. I appointed him as base commandant with the mission to clean up the place, administer it, and see to the distribution and preparation of rations and generally to maintain discipline.

He took no nonsense from anybody. At times he could be quite harsh and I am certain that he would have shot one or two culprits if we were not present at the time. He carried around a big stick, which made painful contact with many an FNLA bottom or back. I was satisfied with Double O, in spite of his war name.

With him also came some more FNLA troops and we could form a third company. This company I gave to a Portuguese, formerly a policeman in Angola, by the name of Costa. Danny and Silva, also Portuguese, were the only two platoon leaders appointed to him.

I had to take away two of Connie's platoon leaders, to create C Company, and to re-allocate one platoon leader from Jack's company to Connie. Each company was therefore one platoon leader short.

Over the rutted sand track from Calais in the south, there arrived a number of Land Rovers and Toyotas, even a tractor driven by a motley crew of former Portuguese troops. Pelissa was leading the procession. He had come to re-occupy his house near the falls, and thus also his one remaining farm in Angola.

With him came a young black woman who turned out to be his common-law wife. She was related to Chipenda, which accounted for Pelissa's close relationship with the FNLA leader.

The crew that came with him, about six or seven strong, looked like gangsters, disguised in Portuguese camouflage, and armed with AK47'S, MI'S, Berettas and even an Armalite or two. I discovered later that they were, in fact, a bunch of gangsters who, under Pelissa's leadership, had robbed several banks, especially in Nova Lisboa, Angola's second biggest city to the north. This then was Pelissa's bodyguard. He had come to stay permanently and to expand his operations in south-eastern Angola.

There is still a lot of ivory and animal skins in these parts, as well as an inexhaustable supply of Rhodesian teak. Pelissa, by climbing in before any of the other Portuguese refugees could make a move, staked his claims to most, if not all, of the bountiful treasures from this region.

His obvious eagerness to get training underway began to make sense. As the days flew by I could detect signs that Pelissa's main concern was to secure south-eastern Angola for FNLA and for himself. He began to interfere more and more with the training and started to drop hints that Mavinga to the north-east, Vila Nova D'Armada and Cuito Cuanavale upstream from M'pupa and even Rivungo on the Cuando River should be secured by driving out MPLA and also UNITA.

At the time we were installed in one wing of his house while his wife, and his foreman called D'Oliviera (rumoured to be the wife's lover) occupied the other wing. His bodyguard slept on the wide gauze-enclosed stoep.

Our personal rations began to disappear and always seemed to end up in Pelissa's kitchen.

The wife took exception to our presence and Pelissa's bodyguard began to sponge on us. They claimed that Pelissa failed to pay them and while we felt sorry for them, we did not have enough to feed them as well.

D'Oliviera made things unpleasant by refusing to attend to minor problems on our vehicles. By this time Pelissa had re-opened and re-equipped the farm workshop, no doubt with looted equipment from elsewhere. The last straw was the stealing of our diesel, which we kept at his house to refuel our vehicles.

We then decided to move out and to establish ourselves in an old hunting camp called Coutada de M'pupa, across the Cuito River and about four kilometres downstream. To get there we had to cross on a ferry or pontoon, which we pulled across the river by hand.

At Coutada de M'pupa we found a former professional hunter in occupation. He had a mulatto wife and two very naughty children and had the very old Afrikaans name of Van Dyk, obviously a descendant of the "Dorsland" Trekkers, although he could not speak English or Afrikaans.

We moved into two of the huts and undertook to supply Van Dyk with diesel and rations, provided he would shoot the odd antelope or so in order to provide fresh meat to a crew that had become somewhat tired of tinned food.

Pelissa had confiscated his one and only drum of diesel so that he could not pump water or run his Land Rover, so to him this was a most excellent arrangement. From then on we had excellent co-operation from Van Dyk and his family until the day we left M'pupa. Mrs Van Dyk, of her own free will, even cooked for us, baked bread and so on.

A final arrival was João and his common-law wife, both mulattoes. João was higher up in the FNLA hierarchy than Double O so that, theoretically, Double O had to be replaced. From the moment I met João, however, I could see that he did not have it in him to control the troops, that in fact the troops may resent him because he had quite a superior pose about him. I therefore made him my second in command and kept Double O on as camp commandant. João was given no particular tasks and only had to look important, which he could do very well, and to act as spokesman between me and Pelissa and any other FNLA leaders who might turn up at M'pupa.

It was not long before an Aztec, similar to one flown by Jules, unexpectedly arrived over M'pupa, but coming from the north and not the south.

We rushed to the airstrip to find a rather large sweaty African, introduced to me as Chipenda himself, Kombuta, the party secretary of Chipenda's FNLA, an American called Cameron, and the white Portuguese pilot awaiting our arrival.

Kombuta I had met once or twice before in Rundu when we discussed the training and equipping of FNLA.

This was the first time I had met Chipenda. He looked quite impressive and evidently was a very eloquent speaker. He also liked his whisky and reportedly suffered from high blood pressure, probably as a consequence of his love of whisky and women.

Pelissa, of course, arrived before we did and we all moved to the coolness of his house to discuss future plans. The discussion between Chipenda and myself did not amount to much because we could not speak each other's language. I gathered from Kombuta, however, that Cameron had been brought along by Chipenda to convince him, Cameron, that the Americans should give support to the FNLA cause.

Cameron and I therefore launched into a discussion from which I gathered that President Gerald Ford was supporting Holden Roberta and that he, Cameron, had direct access to him through Henry Kissinger.

He also told me that the delivery of a "packet" of weapons, ammunition, clothing and rations for 1000 men for a period of six months could quite easily be arranged. M'pupa airstrip, in fact, was ideally situated to accept C-130s from Zaire for clandestine deliveries of all these supplies with maximum security.

I, of course, accepted this proposal, coming as it did out of the blue and from the Americans too. This was the first time that I became aware of American involvement with Holden Roberto's FNLA during their war against Portugal. Roberto seemed to have been their protégé and the horse they were backing at the time. It was possible therefore that the Americans were carrying on with the previous arrangements that existed between them and FNLA.

The FNLA battalion was paraded after completion of our discussions. This time the troops were less raggedly formed in relatively straight ranks and with much more of a soldier-like bearing. Increased rations had filled them out and the uniform greyness of the skin had disappeared. The new uniforms and weapons must have impressed Chipenda, because he launched into an impassioned speech which, I gathered from João, promised a new dawn for Angola, death to all FNLA's enemies, freedom of speech, religion, a capitalist society and so on, in short, the typical speech of any African political leader. He left after numerous "FNLA Oyezs", for Aztec, beaming at me and obviously proud of his new-look army. They took off and disappeared to the north. I never saw or heard from Cameron again.

I wrote a report, however, and got a real stinker in reply, not from the Brigadier but from Pretoria.

"Who gave you the right to approach the Americans for aid or even to make contact with them"? The fact that they came to me and that I never even knew of their existence, somehow escaped Pretoria's attention. I was very firmly told to get on with my training and to leave negotiations with outsiders, especially Americans, to people who knew what it was about and how to do it.

The promised equipment, in spite of discreet inquiries by me, never materialised. I was in particular need of decent mortars, light machine guns, grenade launchers and anti-tank weapons.

Whether it was my inadvertent contact with the Americans that killed the project or whether the Americans were not too impressed with my battalion, I would never know.

My old "spy" now came to me with some rather alarming news. UNITA was planning to take over Calais by force in the next day or two from the direction of Cuangar, using the Cuangar UNITA garrison. The UNITA commander at Cuangar, Johnny Katale, was also an officer in SWAPO and had been expanding SWAPO influence diligently in the area of the Kavango Homeland just across the river. The South African Security Police were also interested in Johnny and his doings, and to bring his influence to a sudden end would not only keep my back door, via Calais, open but would also remove the source of all SWAPO influence in the area. The FNLA-oriented population of Calais was in uproar because they could foresee nothing but indiscriminate slaughter ahead if Johnny should succeed in taking the town.

I therefore rapidly dispatched Jack with his company, half the machine guns under command, to Calais to secure the place against attack by UNITA or SWAPO or both. I also informed my headquarters what I was about to do.

Calais is a small town but with many kraals around it and numerous approaches from the east, west and north. It was quite a problem to defend the place adequately.

When I arrived at Calais, having followed Jack in my Land Cruiser, I therefore set about making a reconnaissance of the area and discussing with Jack the best solution to the defence problem.

We decided that our best chance would be to base the defence on the inner core of Calais town itself, in other words to ignore the outlying kraals. Platoon positions were established to the east, north and west, each position supported by a Vickers machine-gun section. A small reserve was established. Flanks could be tied up because the perimeter was small enough for one rifle company to defend.

Satisfied with our handiwork, and our initiative, I crossed the river to Rundu to make my final report to the Brigadier.

He, however, seemed disturbingly unimpressed with my deployments and plan in general. In fact, the old man ignored me completely and started telling me about military support to UNITA. He had some other officers with him, amongst others Phillip and a fellow known throughout the army as "Kaas".

The discussion turned into planning to fly in brand-new 81 mm mortars, rifles, LMGs and so on to UNITA at Silva Porto where Kaas would act as liaison officer with UNITA. I was very unhappy about this because I could do with some of the equipment.

It was obvious to me that somewhere along the line FNLA had become of lesser importance while UNITA had become the new horse to back. Since I had been at M'pupa over the last month or so, I had become completely out of touch with new developments in Angola. My protestations about UNITA support to SWAPO therefore made no impression whatsoever. Savimbi, in fact, had become the new star in the sky. Chipenda's star was fast waning and he was in any case considered to be nothing but a gangster in the disguise of a freedom fighter controlling a mob that called itself FNLA.

With the first assessment, regarding Chipenda, I had to agree. But the battalion I commanded was rapidly getting shaped into a genuine fighting force, with the FNLA troops becoming loyal to their new South African commanders and beginning to lose their attachment to the old order.

I stopped at Calais on my way to M'pupa and decided to keep the troops in place, just in case Johnny Katale did decide to oust FNLA from Calais. Back at M'pupa we stepped up the training of C Company and the anti-tank platoon, for which I had found a commander in the shape of one of Pelissa's bodyguards who had deserted him and joined our cause.

Shortly afterwards I received a new summons to report to Rundu. This time I flew out and landed one afternoon late, after work, at the airbase. The Brigadier was not available but "Corky", a colonel, wanted to speak to me.

I found him lying on his bed in the officer's quarters. A new formation, combat formation Zulu, had been formed out of combat groups Alpha and Bravo. With this formation we were about to launch an invasion of southern Angola in a week's time to seek out and destroy MPLA.

Alpha, a battalion of mostly ex Portuguese Bushmen "flechas", was commanded by my good friend Delville. Bravo was my renamed FNLA battalion.

Operation Savannah was about to start and UNITA was not to be the enemy after all but our allies in this venture.

FOUR
Off to War

I informed Jack that he and his company could stand down from their mission to defend Calais against a UNITA attack. Instead, they had to concentrate at a point on the northern bank of the Okavango River directly opposite Rundu, which is situated on the South West African side.

My other company commanders and the FNLA commandantes were briefed as far as I could, allowing for the security of the operation.

There were some long faces among the commandantes. One had to keep in mind that less than a year before they themselves were part of FAPLA, the military wing of MPLA, and here they were about to be launched against their old comrades in arms instead of UNITA which, to some, was still the real enemy.

My FNLA intelligence officer gave me a very graphic description of the strength of FAPLA, especially around Sá da Bandeira where the mysterious 122 Stalin Organs, later known to us as the "Red Eye", were deployed on high ground from where they could engage any approaching forces at least 20 kilometres away. The rockets, according to him, were capable of killing between 50 and 100 people on each impact.

At the time I had vaguely heard of the 122 mm Katyusha rockets, knew nothing about their capabilities, however, and was therefore impressed with my 1.0's account of what we could expect. Looking at my platoon of three-inch mortars that could reach 1000 metres, I felt, understandably, somewhat apprehensive of the future.

So, possibly, did some of my commandantes. Double O came to see me. He had received word that his son had died in Mavinga. Could he go to Mavinga to sort out his wife and family, bury his son and join us later, probably at Sá da Bandeira?

Domingos just wanted to go up the river to say goodbye to some friends.

I never saw Double O again, although later on he would appear on the scene in the Mavinga area to cause us some grief and numerous problems.

Domingos stayed away until the day of our departure, which had been delayed. When he turned up at M'pupa in his Land Rover he fully expected us to have left already. He was somewhat surprised to find us still there and not a little put out when I confiscated his Land Rover for the use of my anti-tank platoon. Domingos, being obviously unwilling to go to war, I left in charge of the M'pupa base, the sick, lame and lazy and other non-combatants. There were already some soldiers' dependants settling in the area.

Domingos was unhappy with his assignment, not from a lack of fighting spirit but because he could not yet see MPLA as the enemy. Later on in the unit's history, he too would come to the fore as one of my best and most courageous fighters against SWAPO.

The Brigadier's staff bought some civilian trucks from Portuguese refugees who were stranded on the South West African-Angola border with heaps of worthless escudos and no way of paying their way to Portugal.

By all accounts these unfortunate people were given a pretty square deal by the South African Army in that they received reasonable prices for their vehicles. Later on, there was quite a lot of exploitation of these unfortunate people who, in their desire to leave Africa and having suffered untold miseries and abuse from the hands of all three Angolan movements, took whatever was offered as long as it was in Rands and in cash. Some of these refugees left with all their household goods in the backs of their trucks from deep inside Angola and arrived on the South West African border with nothing, having been robbed at roadblocks along the way of everything but the clothes they were standing up in.

It was also not unusual for mothers and daughters to have been raped, almost as a drill, at roadblocks as the families made their way southwards.

During all this the Portuguese Army, under "new management" kept a hands-off posture and nowhere in Angola did they lift a finger to protect their own citizens against the undisciplined "liberation movements".

So we acquired some rather splendid ten-ton six-wheel- and four-wheel-drive trucks as our transport and we promptly dubbed them vegetable lorries. In South Africa many Portuguese are market gardeners – an occupation at which they excel. They convey their vegetables to markets or to shops by the lorry load. Thus the nickname.

We therefore became motorised on paper as we still had to collect our vehicles in Rundu. The Brigadier sent a fleet of Unimogs to collect my troops at M'pupa and to transport them to their concentration area at Calais.

So in due course close on 600 FNLA troops, all equipped with brand-new rifles and suitably attired in jungle-green fatigues, concentrated just across the river from Rundu at a point where the houses in Rundu were crowding right up to the edge of a cliff dropping off into the Okavango River below.

The already nervous folk in Rundu were somewhat alarmed at the unidentified black troops camping on the other side of the river almost, it seemed, at the end of their splendid tropical gardens. Because of the many rumours and counter-rumours over the past year of conflict in southern Angola, they did not know who were actually in occupation at any one time in Calais. They were also completely uninformed of our imminent advance into Angola.

Also with our troops' complete disregard for modesty, some ladies could not enjoy their shady verandahs while the troops were bathing just across from them. I was therefore summoned to Rundu headquarters and told to move myself and my "mob" away from the river and out of sight of the worthy Rundu "burghers" and their women folk. I was also told in no unclear terms that South African troops would be deployed along the river, and if one of my troops put a foot across he would be dispatched to the next world in no uncertain manner.

Bravo Group did not therefore start off the war esteemed

very highly by the South Africans, except for the few of us who actually worked with them.

We were beginning to develop a tentative regard for our unpredictable troops and were therefore highly indignant at the obvious prejudice toward our unit and the slight, intended or otherwise, to our troops. I complained to the Brigadier and assured him that our troops were under full control, but prudently moved them back from the riverbank into thick vegetation where the inhabitants of Rundu could not see them without resorting to their binoculars.

My biggest problem, though, was to keep them out of the kraals surrounding Calais. A pass system was arranged and patrols organised to police the area. We thus kept contact between the troops and the local population at a manageable level and made certain that no troops were missing when we finally started.

The engineers supplied us one dark night, by means of a raft, with loads of ammunition and rations for our march to the north. The engineer officer in charge of the operation had no inkling of the identity of the white soldiers he was conferring with on the banks of the Okavango. Although we knew each other well, I persisted in conducting my conversation with him in very broken English. He obviously thought that we were Portuguese mercenaries and referred to us, when speaking to his own men, in a somewhat unflattering manner. He clearly had no love for the Portuguese as a fighting nation.

We were re-supplied and plans were finally made to move the whole of the Zulu invasion force westwards along the river to Katitwi, at the point where the Okavango River meets the SWA border, from where the invasion proper would start.

I had enough vehicles on the Angolan side to ferry Jack and his company, via Cuangar, to Katitwi. The rest of Bravo Group had to cross the river early one morning where we were loaded into our trucks and proceeded westwards to Katitwi on the South West African side of the river.

UNITA being our allies, Jack received strict instructions not to pick a fight with Johnny Katale at Cuangar, but to bypass

Cuangar if need be. In the end, Johnny and his crew must have been overwhelmed when they saw Jack's company driving through the town, FNLA banners flying from each truck and the troops singing their FNLA songs at full blast, especially when they spotted the miserable UNITA occupying force peering apprehensively at them from the depths of the dark verandahs or from around corners.

The trucks in my group were very soon festooned with FNLA banners and FNLA songs could be heard up and down the convoy. Luckily nobody took it into his head to fire the normal joyful shots into the air, so prevalent a custom among them only a few short weeks before. Discipline was just beginning to show among the troops.

The Kavango population were astonished. It must have come as a great surprise to see hundreds of well-armed Angolan soldiers driving through their country.

Maybe they thought that the war in Angola had finally got so out of hand that one faction, FNLA, had decided to invade South West Africa. At any event, they stood gaping along the roadside, some tentatively waving but mostly quiet and possibly apprehensive of the future. We arrived late that afternoon at Katitwi. Jack, who had left the previous night, was nowhere in sight but then the road along the north bank was atrocious. We had received no indication that he met with trouble at Cuangar. We therefore pulled off the road and prepared for a night laager, our last in South African-controlled territory for a long time.

Zulu headquarters arrived with Corky in charge and Willie as his principal staff officer responsible for operational planning.

Then Delville arrived with his Bushmen. These Bushmen looked very unhappy when they saw my FNLA, ex-MPLA, troops and clutched their rifles somewhat tighter when they met their old enemies from the Portuguese war. I dare say some of them surreptitiously eased off their safety catches, just in case the whole thing was an elaborate trap which their own white officers were too stupid to see through.

Delville had his job cut out to convince his troops that my black troops were "on side", that the real enemy, FAPLA, was still ahead of us some days into the future and that the FAPLA encamped on the opposite side of the road from them, were not really FAPLA but FNLA who, in this war, were also after the common enemy, namely FAPLA. They therefore could relax and must not pick a quarrel with my men and I would make sure that my troops would keep their distance.

This confused the Bushmen even more and Delville's explanation cut no ice with them. An enemy remains an enemy for ever and a friend remains a friend for ever. There were no half measures and they felt that the white men must be pitied because they could not see the error of their ways. They could not accept that a mere handful of white men could go to war with 600 terrorists, the composition of Bravo Group, and were convinced that I and my white officers would get our throats cut.

Our last night was spent dining with Vossie. Zulu headquarters and the Alpha and Bravo Group headquarters were invited to a splendid dinner.

Vossie was in control of the refugees just across the border, from Katitwi, inside Angola. He had to feed them, give them medical aid and handle their documentation while they awaited passage to Portugal or to emigrate to South Africa.

To assist him he had a few national servicemen. He had a thankless job, with numerous Portuguese constantly clamouring for assistance and his undivided attention and sometimes not averse to attempting a bribe if they could not get what they wanted.

Vossie had a small tented camp on high ground overlooking the river and the refugee camp. We turned up for dinner and found beautifully laid tables, with silver and wine glasses, and white tablecloths, unexpected in the middle of the hot and dusty bush.

While we were having our pre-dinner drinks, an apparition appeared from the direction of a tent, a little way off, floating along in a white evening dress. Vossie, it turned out, had an attractive young nursing sister assisting him in his onerous tasks. Later she was known as the Angel of Calais. After a moment of stunned silence, we recovered from our surprise and she became the centre of attention as the men flocked around her like bees around a honeypot. Delville, however, took over the show while the rest of us resumed our pre-dinner beers, ragging Vossie about the "difficult" circumstances under which he had to execute his assignment while we, fortunate fellows, only had to cope with the dust, flies, FAPLA and other uncertainties of the campaign ahead of us.

There was a slightly superior attitude and a thankfulness that the "powers that be" did not see fit to saddle any of us with a bunch of Portuguese refugees. For us it was to be the smoke and flame of the battlefield and the more wine we consumed, the more misty our eyes became with the anticipation of the battle ahead. For most it would be the first time.

The next morning we mounted our vehicles and the invasion began. Alpha Group was leading.

We followed the track northwards to Caiundu, through the refugee camp just beyond the border where in their hundreds they were cheering us on to victory and "death to FAPLA and communism". Maybe they had visions of South Africa restoring Angola to them with the pleasant lives they had led as Portuguese Colonialists.

By this time everybody knew that South Africa was invading Angola, except the South Africans back home. The Portuguese refugees certainly were not fooled and, after a day or two, neither were the surprised inhabitants of Kavango.

South Africa, for the second time in its history, was invading a foreign territory. The first invasion was during the First World War when the Union invaded the then German South West Africa.

FIVE
First Clash – UNITA

We did not get very far before we had to stop near a place called Catambue, barely across the border.

Delville was having problems with the flood plain of the Okavango River in the area of Tandaue. The road between Caiundo and Kititwi was still under construction when the Portuguese pulled out of Angola, dropping tools as they went. Fortunately, they left a perfectly sound bulldozer which Delville now used to pull his trucks through the thick mud of the flood plain while trying to bypass a particularly sandy and treacherous-looking stretch of road.

Disenchanted and frustrated we walked up and down the river. We had a wash, contemplated a swim but decided against it on account of the crocodiles, and investigated a "firewater still" which a local inhabitant must have left in a hurry when he saw hundreds of fierce-looking FNLA troops descending on his small kraal. The freshly picked monkey oranges and nuts, commonly used for distilling the stuff, was lying all around his place of work. Unfortunately, there was no sign of the finished product, unless some of my troops had managed to get there first and liberated the stuff.

Corky and his headquarters pulled up. Compared to my headquarters, his was quite elaborate, but it seemed rather scant to perform the functions of a brigade headquarters.

Firstly he had Willie, a gunner, as his principal staff officer. Then he had Shylock, an engineer, as his logistics officer. Dave was his intelligence officer. Shylock and Dave went as far as Sá da Bandeira and were then lost to Corky.

To give his headquarters some substance he was subsequently joined by Uncle Sarel as communications officer and a driver that could speak Portuguese and English when he arrived at Pereira de Eça. At Sá da Bandeira Dries and an assistant, Leon, replaced Dave as intelligence team and they had with them a very useful retired Pide inspector as interrogator. Piet became logistics officer.

My headquarters consisted of myself and Paul, my Portuguese-speaking radio operator cum driver. He knew very little about a radio set and also ignored the bare rudiments of safe driving. Paul therefore sat next to me, as a passenger, with the headsets of the various radios slung around his neck. More often than not he was fast asleep. I almost always had to wake him up when I heard somebody calling us on one of the nets. It invariably resulted in Paul answering on the wrong net first and then frantically shouting into each microphone before finally getting the right one, which always seemed to be the last one.

I did the driving as I could not bear to see my "cut-down" and sportified Land Cruiser in Paul's hands.

We slept the night at Catambue. Corky was getting restless because the longer we took to get to Pereira de Eça, our first objective, the better the chances would be that MPLA would become aware of our advance. They would have more time to dig in and properly prepare the town against our assault from the north, this being our intention.

None of us, and I the least of all, looked forward to fighting through a town with badly trained troops, not yet proven in battle.

Corky was instructed to move as far as Caiundo and then further on the road, still under construction, to Pereira de Eça. He was informed by the higher headquarters that the road under construction was in an excellent condition and that the aim of the move was to create the impression that the force attacking Pereira de Eça came from the north-east and not from the south. However, Delville's problems further to the north bode ill for the future.

Finally Corky decided that I must bypass Delville in order to make Caiundo before dark.

We set off cheerfully and made good time to Tandaue where we found Delville's vehicles stuck, in a long train, in the mud. The Tandaue is an omuramba that joins the Okavango from the west. A quick inspection showed that off the road the going was very soggy, swampy in fact, because the flood plains and the beds of omurambas close to the river flood plains act as sponges for the heavy rains that fall from November onwards. Even at the end of the dry season the plains are still very much swamps of mud and isolated pools of water.

We therefore stuck to the road. I gave strict instructions that nobody was to stop for vehicles getting stuck in the loose sand but to push on until we had passed the bad patch. Delville's bulldozer would pull clear those vehicles that got stuck.

We charged on in spite of the looseness of the sand and we all got through without mishap.

Long before sunset we arrived at Caiundo and laagered on the eastern side of the bridge. Caiundo was in the hands of UNITA. Rumour also had it that there was a SWAPO base 12 kilometres upstream on the eastern bank, with the knowledge and connivance of UNITA, of course.

When Corky turned up with his headquarters I proposed to him that a night attack on his base would be a splendid way to shake my men down for the no doubt fierce battles awaiting us in the future.

He was not amused, possibly because we were joined by a Major Katahale from UNITA who would act as liaison officer between us and "them". He must not be confused with Johnny Katale from Cuangar who, at this stage, was probably still in that vicinity creating problems for the police in the Kavango by expanding SWAPO's influence while most of the army was concentrating on Angola.

Katahale was well dressed and smart in camouflaged fatigues and looked rather more refined and educated than my FNLA riff-raff. In fact, it was quickly obvious that he had no intention of associating with me, my officers or the battle group. He stuck to headquarters.

Delville also had some unflattering things to say about Katahale after he met him, probably because Bushmen were even lower in Katahale's esteem than FNLA troops.

Katahale no doubt assured Corky that there were no SWAPO in the area. My offer to send a patrol, just to make sure, was not taken up, so we turned in for the night, rather disgruntled.

The next morning I was told to move to Serpa Pinto and from there to Artur de Paiva to reconnoitre the route. Serpa Pinto was in the hands of FNLA and Artur de Paiva in the hands of UNITA. I therefore decided to take João and to go with my Land Cruiser, leaving the rest to catch up later if Corky decided to take this longer route.

Delville had to reconnoitre the road still under construction towards Pereira de Eça, which was also the shorter route, but less likely to take the weight of our heavy lorries.

We set off on a beautiful tarred road at a great clip and reached Serpa in record time. We turned west onto a good dirt road, parallel to the railway line from Moçâmedes, towards Artur de Paiva without refuelling at Serpa.

The terrain was much more bushy and greener than further south. There was plenty of water and we passed numerous well-constructed kraals, mostly flying the UNITA flag, with populations that seemed well fed and content. We did not dare to stop, however, as both João and myself were sporting FNLA badges on our forage caps.

I turned back at Cuchi for Serpa Pinto as we were getting low on fuel and the road as far as Artur de Paiva was obviously in excellent condition.

Serpa was then a very pleasant fair-sized town, still largely undamaged by the war, situated on the Cuebe River which divided the town in two.

Chipenda, my boss, lived in a very large pink house, set in beautiful gardens with palms and all sorts of flowering tropical trees and shrubs, the river being at the bottom end of a vast expanse of lawn. He was not at home – not that I had any intention of calling on him.

The Mafia gang from Calais were there, however, and also Kombuta, FNLA's secretary. We therefore quickly rustled up some diesel and left for Caiundo. Seen off by cheerful high-ranking FNLA officials who were already, in their minds, counting the escudos that would stream into their own private coffers once we had dealt with MPLA.

I met Corky and Zulu Force on the way to Caiundo. Delville came back with a negative report on the state of the Pereira de Eça road. Some of my troops were still in Caiundo, so I pushed on south, collected the tail end of my unit and headed north again for Cuchi.

Just beyond Cuchi we caught up with the rest where they were in laager for the night.

It was an exceedingly cold night because we laagered on the side of an omuramba and not on high ground as we should have done. We were therefore glad to "saddle up" the next morning, and with my battle group leading, we entered Artur de Paiva and made contact with the first roadblocks.

They were UNITA-manned and in spite of explanations by Paul, they refused to let us through.

So we took matters into our own hands and drove through, scattering drums, barriers and UNITA troops in all directions. They did not dare to show any fight because several hundred FNLA eyes, burning with suppressed desire to come to grips with UNITA, glared at them from our vegetable lorries.

Once more we crossed the Okavango, this time southwards across an iron bridge.

The road, although dusty, remained good, and we finally pulled into Techamutete for the night – the site of the biggest iron-ore mines in Angola.

We had passed Cassinga 16 kilometres to the north without stopping. If I had known that later on in life Cassinga would play a very important part in my military career, I would no doubt have stopped for a while and taken careful note of the terrain and town. As it turned out, I could hardly remember passing through the place.

Techamutete had a large dam serving the mines, which were out of production at the time. So we washed, topped up with water and reconnoitred the nearby landing strip. The terrain was getting drier again as we moved southwards, water was getting scarcer so that even muddy dam water could not be sneered at.

We heard from the locals that we were running out of UNITA-controlled areas and that around Cuvelai we would be entering FAPLA territory. So we were extra careful when moving off the next morning, still leading Force Zulu. I had an advance patrol consisting of Connie in a Land Rover fitted with twin .30 Brownings, another similar vehicle as his number two and one platoon just behind him for immediate support. I followed in my Land Cruiser with two Land Rovers, each with two Vickers machine guns in the back. Behind me came the mortar platoon, quite far to the front of the column because the range of our crapped-out three-inch mortars was only 1000 metres. The rest of the column followed in respective companies with the echelon vehicles bringing up the rear. The column probably stretched over five kilometres or more.

I always tried to have as much firepower as possible as far forward as possible. In this way any resistance to the advance could be overcome quickly, provided my machine gunners, mortar men and manoeuvre elements in the advance patrols were quick off the mark.

Our advance was relatively slow because resistance was expected around every corner, and any high ground commanding the dirt road to the south was viewed with the greatest suspicion and with some apprehension.

Although dry, the bush was pretty thick and visibility was rarely more than a hundred metres. We could therefore expect to come under fairly accurate fire at short ranges. I did not envy Connie, but he seemed to be happy with his machine guns and in his element to lead the column and therefore to be the first to make contact.

We did not reach Cuvelai before last light.

The advance patrols got up to the bridge crossing the dry Cuvelai River, just to the north of the town, and settled down to watch the buildings on the other side while I deployed the rest of my unit, ready for an all-out assault if necessary.

I moved forward to have a look at the town reportedly in the hands of FAPLA. The town stretched southwards in two rows of houses on both sides of the single main street, well lit with street lamps. We had checked the bridge for demolition charges, but there were none.

I sent a patrol through to secure the southern end of the bridge and soon they reappeared with a big camouflaged soldier, unarmed and with hands raised above the head.

Through Paul he told me that he was a UNITA officer, that the town was in the hands of UNITA, and that he had been sent by his commander to make contact with us.

I therefore detailed Nel's platoon to come with us, and with the UNITA officer in the Land Cruiser with me, we warily made our way to the UNITA garrison, housed in the old Portuguese "quartel" on the southern outskirts. According to my new "friend" there were about 40 of them. The nearest FAPLA were in Mupa, the next town along the road to Pereira de Eça.

Nel moved his troops on both sides of the street, every one as alert as they would ever be, not having any trust in UNITA.

Suddenly the street lights went out and we were left in total darkness. It suited me because I never liked to be lit up while hostile eyes could watch from the darkness beyond.

We finally drew level with the quartel on our left in an open space with two rows of impenetrable sisal on our right. We were in a perfect killing ground as our rear, the direction of any possible cover would be cut off by sisal, and the street to the north and south afforded no cover at all.

Suddenly all hell broke loose. Tracers came streaming from the quartel buildings about 50 paces to our left, interspersed with the odd 60 millimetre mortar thumping in the fields behind us. The bullets crackling overhead indicated that they were, fortunately, and as usual, firing high.

I turned round to shoot my "UNITA" friend who had obviously led us deliberately into an ambush, but he was gone – whether through the sisal, I would never know.

My troops were all down in the middle of the road and I pulled them back to behind the camber where there was a certain amount of protection. Their eyes were white in the darkness and all seemed to stare at me, expecting no doubt a decision of some sort. Not one was returning the fire from the quartel. So much for our training!

"Shoot, you bastards! Look at the enemy and not at me! Shoot, damn you!" My English must have broken through the paralysis of their minds.

Slowly the returning fire began to build up, high of course, but nevertheless to a satisfactory level so that everybody's morale began to pick up. I was meanwhile trying to make some sense out of the enemy dispositions. There was a particularly bothersome machine gun firing from a smaller building set slightly back on the UNITA right. To the front there were two large buildings ablaze, lighting up the whole scene, including us behind our miserable cover.

I had brought one rocket launcher team with me, manned by the ex-Portuguese commando who was also my anti-tank platoon leader. I instructed him to put a rocket into the small building housing the machine gun.

Suddenly there was an almighty bang, clouds of dust, smoke and flame. It seemed that something heavy, possibly an 82 mm mortar shell, had fallen right among us.

I could see nothing, not even the burning thatch roofs, as there was no wind at all to clear the smoke and dust. Gradually though I began to make out my intrepid rocketeer on my left. He was covered in dust, as no doubt I was, but he was kneeling with the rocket launcher firmly placed on the ground at a 45 degree angle.

"What the hell are you doing? You must aim at the little building!" As the smoke cleared I pointed vigorously at the still firing machine gun. In broken English he told me that he was using "high angle" fire as they used to do in the Portuguese Army.

"You are not in the bloody Portuguese Army. Now do as I tell you. See that building with the machine gun?"

"Yes!"

"Now shoot at it by aiming your bloody launcher directly at the building!"

Now rocket launchers work on the principle of a back blast that cancels out the recoil when a rocket is launched out of the tube. The tube at the back is open, and usually flared, this particular one being a 3.1 rocket launcher, which allows a tremendous amount of flame and gas to escape to the rear. Standing behind one of these can be highly dangerous when it is fired. Men have been killed that way.

This fellow proceeded to reload, and while I was looking at the burning buildings, noting that UNITA fire was decreasing, there was another tremendous bang, smoke, flame, dust and even pebbles flying about.

This time I could taste the blood in the back of my throat. My ears rang and my eyes, mouth and nose were clogged with dust.

He had done it again because faintly in the distance I could hear a thump as the rocket finally returned to earth "from outer space".

"Get the hell out of here! Bugger off! Vamoose, you stupid bastard!"

Very indignantly he picked up his rocket launcher and strolled down the road to the north, still under fire by UNITA. He vanished into the dark, never to be used by me again in any fighting capacity. I finally got rid of him in Sá da Bandeira.

Our fire was becoming effective. Even the machine gun had pulled out and fire seemed to be coming from a position beyond the burning buildings. Obviously the time had come for an assault.

Full of determination and aggression I therefore shouted in my best carrying voice "Advance!" while tentatively moving forward myself. Not a movement from anybody up and down the line.

"Advance, you bastards!" Just white eyes staring at me. In the end Nel and I were compelled to move up and down the line, literally picking some up by the scruff of their necks and the seat of their pants, running forward with them, dumping them and coming back for more.

Kicking and swearing finally got them as far as the first line of buildings. UNITA was now shooting at us from an embankment on the eastern side of the quartel.

We took up position, returned fire and promptly set a second line of buildings ablaze. It was less troublesome to start the second phase of the assault, possibly the first assault these troops had ever been in.

We reached the embankment, but UNITA had vanished into the darkness beyond, leaving us in sole possession of a merrily burning quartel.

Searching the place produced no dead bodies or discarded equipment, just the odd bits of uniform, some rations and lots of rubbish. The place stank of burnt thatch, cordite and the usual human excreta which was normally found on the outskirts of all bases, be they UNITA, FNLA or FAPLA.

I was livid. UNITA had deliberately led us into an ambush and I reported back in this vein to Corky, via the rider, that I would not mind having a word with Katahale.

Meanwhile I heard from the local population that UNITA had withdrawn to a position ten kilometres east of Cuvelai, to a farming complex. I therefore dispatched Danny and Silva with two platoons with strict instructions to sort out UNITA once and for all.

We proceeded to warm ourselves at the burning buildings and reflected on UNITA's treachery. The troops were taking up a position of all-round defence around the quartel. All our vehicles had been moved into the centre.

By first light Danny and Silva returned with their tired platoons. There was no sign of UNITA.

Jack came up with a RPG-7 which had been found under a tree by one of the troops, obviously, according to him, a piece of equipment abandoned by UNITA. At last we had something to show for our labours and for our moments of fright.

A little while later a troop from the anti-tank platoon pitched up. Had anybody seen his RPG-7 which he had left under a tree? So much for our first war loot.

And so ended our first contact of the Savannah Campaign, a skirmish with UNITA which did not ease our minds about

UNITA as an ally in this campaign. In fact, Corky had his job cut out to keep me away from the throat of the UNITA commander of Cuvelai when later in the day he pitched up to sheepishly pay his respects to his new allies.

In retrospect, probably nobody had told him of the new developments in Angola.

SIX
Pereira de Eça

We left Cuvelai at about eight the next morning, with our foes of the night before picking up the pieces and re-establishing themselves as a viable garrison, this time in roofless buildings.

At least my troops had their first taste of war and in the telling and retelling of the previous night's events, their stature increased enormously while that of UNITA decreased to vanishing point. FAPLA, or anybody else, had a wild cat by the tail if they were to tangle with this FNLA bunch.

One positive aspect of the skirmish which was driven home for the first time to the minds of my FNLA troops was the fact that their white commanders were perfectly willing to take the punch with them. When the lead was flying about, they did not sit back some distance away from the scene of battle while telling their men to get on with it, which was the fashion of their old FNLA commandantes.

The result was that the first buds of loyalty, barely detectable still, began to poke to the surface, a loyalty more to the commanders than to the FNLA cause. Chipenda in his pink house in Serpa Pinto was beginning to become somewhat more distant and removed from his FNLA army.

We headed south for Mupa, a little village boxed in between some fairly high hills to the east and a dry riverbed in the west.

The hills were obvious delaying positions, beautifully placed to hold up our advance and difficult to flank to the east because of the thick bush.

Nothing happened, however, as we drove cautiously into the village from the north. At the southern end, where there were some stores, we met unexpectedly with two Land Rovers full of FAPLA who unashamedly left their vehicles in unseemly haste, even before we could open fire, and disappeared into the bush. The result was two reasonably serviceable Land Rovers added to our fleet, something most welcome as we began to realise that we would have to rely on what we could capture in this war. Our logistics had not yet caught up with us, and probably never would satisfy our basic needs anyway, even if it did catch up.

We moved further southwards, faster than the day before, as a certain feeling of élan was taking root among the men.

The next town of consequence would be Evale, reportedly strongly held by FAPLA.

With Connie in front, we made for it at a cracking pace past a mission station and then, suddenly, into an ambush.

An RPG-7 was fired at Connie's Land Rover, but luckily the rocket was a dud. He only sustained a huge dent on the left-hand side, but lots of small-arms fire was coming his way.

Connie returned fire from his twin Brownings very effectively, at the same time shouting for mortar support. Some fire was also coming from the right side of the road, which he could not deal with.

Oupa and his mortars dismounted and came into action with their rickety yokes, trying to frighten FAPLA without frightening our own troops. They succeeded because FAPLA to the front of the column soon began to pack up and leave the scene of battle, thus reducing the fire on our advance patrols.

I was meanwhile about level with Connie, but lying in a ditch alongside the road, trying to keep a semblance of control over events by deploying Jack and his company in case a sweep was necessary, when a tremendous firefight broke out in the rear.

It was, quite honestly, the biggest and the noisiest scrap I had ever heard in my life, away from a cinema screen.

Costa, my C Company commander, informed me that they were being attacked by FAPLA from both flanks and that Zulu headquarters was also under fire.

We were still dealing with FAPLA to the front, and already I had visions of our column of troops being wiped out in true

Vietnam style such as the time when the Viet Minh caught a whole mobile column of French troops in a pass and virtually exterminated all of them over a prolonged period of fighting.

As I could not move because of the lead flying about, I decided to deal with Connie's problem first before paying attention to Costa's problem.

Soon Oupa's effective mortar fire had driven off FAPLA all along Connie's front and the fighting died down. I therefore felt it was reasonably safe to move down the column to see for myself what the situation was.

The fire to the rear, however, was also beginning to slacken off, probably because Charlie Company was beginning to run out of ammunition.

I found Corky and his headquarters in a ditch alongside the road, taking cover against lead flying in all directions. Charlie Company was spread out on both sides, roughly in two halves, pumping rounds away at each other. Luckily they were doing this mostly with eyes closed and with barrels pointing almost straight up into the sky.

There were no FAPLA in sight.

It took some doing to stop all shooting which could only be achieved by walking down the centre of the road and shouting at both sides to cease fire.

Finally both sides stopped more from lack of ammunition than from my efforts and very sheepishly got up to move to their trucks. I could not, however, blame C Company because in our short period of training they had had the least training of all. All I could do was to have a heart to heart talk with Costa.

Unfortunately, it placed them in the almost permanent position of reserve company while they served with me with unfortunate results as we shall see later on. They never really got down to some proper soldiering under fire.

Zulu headquarters also got their baptism of fire, albeit from our own forces in no half-hearted fashion. Corky was somewhat sarcastic about our display of unsolicited firepower, but it did not seem to put his nose out of joint too much. I think he understood our problems, even if we did not understand his as commander of a largely untried force of Africans and Bushmen, surely a nightmare to any military commander who treats war as a serious business.

We swept the bush on both sides of the road and found some dead FAPLA, plus one wounded who was promptly passed on for interrogation and to our doctor for medication. We collected a few PPSHs, AK-47s and a number of Russian helmets which appeared on the heads of some of the troops, Robbie included. He looked quite silly with the large helmet falling over his ears while he peered out at the world from underneath the brim with bright shining eyes and a perpetual grin on his face. Robbie was driving for Connie and he was obviously enjoying the war.

The advance restarted. We still had about ten kilometres to go to Evale, and what we had bumped into was obviously an outpost.

Cautiously the column snaked forward with Connie leading in his converted Land Rover. He stood crouching behind his guns swinging the barrels from side to side, with the irrepressible Robbie driving carefully on the side of the road for maximum cover. The road itself was built up to get clear of the large sheets of water that collect on the almost billiard table level surface during the rainy season.

I similarly drove on the opposite side of the road a little back from Connie and had no intention of attracting the first shots.

Oupa moved his mortars in bounds, half the platoon at a time, and Fingers stayed close behind me with the two Land Rovers and their Vickers machine guns at the alert in the back.

We moved slowly and cautiously, eyes scanning the thick bush with apprehension and expectancy. I intended to get about two kilometres from Evale and, if we had not yet bumped into FAPLA, to do a company assault on the town, using Jack's company.

Just when I decided to stop the advance, Connie hit a contact from the right-hand side of the road, my side. He luckily was on the left with the road giving him good cover.

We quickly went into action, Oupa opening up with his mortars on the right-hand side of the road and Fingers and Connie pumping away with their machine guns.

Jack dismounted and moved his platoons up at the double into an assault position on the right-hand side of the road.

Our performance was getting polished and the troops were beginning to move with some alacrity and with some understanding, in spite of the language barrier.

As Jack moved forward towards the town, I leapfrogged the fire base, that is the mortars and machine guns, forward as well. Charlie Company, at the rear of the column, did not fire a single shot, probably because they had no ammunition left.

Soon the buildings of the town came into view with an MPLA flag flying briskly in the afternoon breeze over the most important-looking building.

FAPLA fired some RPG-7 rockets into the air to burst above our heads scattering some shrapnel. Otherwise their fire was desultory and soon died down when Jack hit the edge of the town.

His troops went through clearing the houses on the right side of the main street. Connie took his leading platoon and cleared the few houses to the left.

FAPLA had pulled out and were no doubt heading for Pereira de Eça. Some vehicles were heard to start up and to disappear rapidly southwards.

So we had Evale in our hands plus the FAPLA's flag, which would look good on the walls of a mess or pub back home.

Corky decided to call a halt and so we laagered just to the south of Evale for the night. There was no water, the bush being as dry as a bone, and no wells in sight. So, very thirsty we turned in for the night. It had been a hot and an eventful day. Apart from Charlie Company's performance, I was satisfied with the way the troops were settling down under fire. Connie, of course, was an absolute marvel. He was later to get the Honoris Crux for his actions on this day. His calmness and his rapid reaction with devastating firepower from his guns while under accurate fire at ranges no greater than ten metres showed courage which had to be rewarded. In fact, the reason why the

RPG-7 rocket that hit him never exploded was because it was fired from less than 15 metres, the distance it had to travel before it could arm itself.

Delville would lead the next morning so I slept peacefully until 0300 hours when my black troops started to get up, noisily as always, to make fires all over the place and to braai meat from goats which they had captured the previous day. I tried to carry on sleeping but it was no use, so long before daybreak I was sipping a mug of coffee and conferring with my company commanders.

Delville and his Bushmen passed us just after daybreak in a cloud of dust, from the rear, to take the lead. We gave them enough space to get ahead before we mounted our trucks for the final approach to our first major target Pereira da Eça, now known as Ongiva.

Delville moved cautiously to the next village, Anhanca, a possible delaying position for FAPLA. I remember that he picked up a scrap there. It was out of earshot for us, being now right at the back of the column recovering our nerve for the severe test we were expecting at Pereira da Eça.

Towards sundown we pulled into a laager about five kilometres short of Pereira da Eça. We were going to stay the night in laager and would launch an attack on the town by about 0800 hours, moving out for the assault by first light.

Corky briefed us on a sand model and a very large air photo. The town stretched roughly two kilometres from east to west on both sides of a main street, in which several rows of houses were found on both sides. Some kraals were situated on the northern outskirts and in my sector. I was given half the town north of the main road as my objective and also the airfield beyond, which had to be taken to facilitate resupplying of the whole of the Zulu Force.

Delville was given the southern half and, in addition, had to send a strong patrol to Namacunde and Santa Clara to secure the tar road leading north from the SWA border.

Gert, the commander of 2 Military sub-area, was waiting just across the border at Santa Clara to deliver to us two troops of armoured cars once junction had been made between him and Delville.

Having been a keen student of war all my life, it seemed to me that a mini El Alamein would be in order. I intended using two companies in the attack: Jack's company to clear the town and Connie's company to clear the kraals to the north. Costa's Charlie Company would be in reserve.

Where it resembled Alamein was in the employment of the mortars. I had read about the old-fashioned "rolling barrage" and decided that this would be just the role for Oupa and his mortars to play. We would deliver a curtain of steel behind which the attacking infantry could advance in relative safety.

There was, of course, the small matter of extremely rickety yokes which did not auger well for the accuracy one would expect when putting down a "rolling barrage" of mortar fire.

I expected a FAPLA attack during the night, being laagered so closely to town, but nothing happened. We arose long before dawn and prepared for what we thought would be a desperate fight. I have always looked on fighting in built up areas with some loathing.

At first light the companies advanced on foot to the start line and by 0800 hours, so-called "H hour", we crossed the start line in plain sight of the nearest buildings.

The town is rather large for Angola and is the provincial capital of Cunene Province. We had a number of substantial buildings in our sector, including a cathedral and a multi-storeyed administration building.

Oupa opened up with his mortars a bare 100 metres in front of the advancing infantry with a curtain of black smoke and deep red flashes as the first salvo arrived.

To the left a rocket started up where Delville was engaging FAPLA with rifles and light mortars.

I followed just behind the infantry in my Land Cruiser trying to keep our advance co-ordinated with Delville's on our left.

The fight was not one-sided as my troops began to receive incoming mortar fire. They, of course, were quick to blame our own mortars remembering the dodgy yokes.

But one could see the difference in smoke from the explosions. Scarcely 20 metres from me a bomb exploded in a cloud of white smoke and an instantaneous brilliant flash, typical post-Second World War explosives. One of my troops did cartwheels in the explosion and dropped lifeless to the ground.

The Second World War three-inch mortar bombs, on the other hand, were exploding with black smoke and deep red, almost orange, flashes.

Delville was also receiving incoming mortar fire and I had my job cut out to convince him, and his troops, that it was not our mortars which were shooting off target.

Looking back to the start line I could see Oupa running around from tube to tube checking sight settings, clouting the odd mortarman from time to time and generally making sure that his platoon would perform well. Soon I had to bound them forward six mortars at a time.

The town had seen fighting before, so there was a fair amount of damage when we started. My mortars did not improve the look of the place. Unfortunately, some bombs went through the roof of the cathedral and did some damage to the rather smallish but beautifully built whitewashed church, the most imposing building in town and the only piece of architecture worth looking at.

The enemy's resistance was very weak to start off with, apart from their mortar shelling, and soon the fight died down to relative silence, broken by the odd clatter of automatics here and there. Oupa had ceased fire and my troops reached the western side of town intact with very few casualties.

I went with Connie's company to secure the airport about eight kilometres beyond. There was no resistance there, but a few civilian light planes were found parked undamaged on the apron. They would come in handy later.

The field was big enough, with a tarred runway, to take the latest jet fighter planes so now, for the first time, we could fly in supplies by C-130 transports. It was therefore a great boon to us and to our limited logistical capability.

Delville cleared the road as far south as Santa Clara and soon we saw the welcome sight of eight Eland armoured cars, the same make basically as Panhards, entering the town from the south. I was disappointed that they were a mixed bunch of 90 mm and 60 mm cars, the latter being a mortar instead of a gun. I would have preferred the 90 mm guns because of the devastating punch the Eland-90 carries. I have always been a great admirer of firepower: the bigger the gun, the better the effect.

We found a hospital reasonably well stocked and a resident medic who claimed to be a doctor. Soon a medical system was established to treat both our wounded and the local population which was riddled with all sorts of nasty diseases. We could not evacuate FNLA wounded to SWA, because of the security problem, so it was essential to leave them behind in Pereira de Eça where they would now be receiving adequate attention.

Small quantities of weapons and ammunition were found. More important were the few vehicles we could confiscate to expand the mobility of our units. We had to carry both troops and equipment on the same vehicles with some odd results, the troops perching on top of a load consisting of a bottom layer of ammunition and explosives, a second layer of personal equipment and rations and a third layer of ready-to-use ammunition, water bottles and the day's rations.

On my way to Zulu headquarters I came across a Bushman trying to start a virtually brand-new Lancia – part of the war loot of Delville's battalion. When I passed the same way later I found the beautiful Lancia completely wrecked against the side of a building. The Bushman obviously could not cope with the problem of driving a car. Delville's reaction was unprintable.

The Brigadier arrived by helicopter to brief us. We would replenish ammunition and fuel before moving on. For food we had to live off the fat of the land, and the land hereabouts was not particularly fat.

He also briefed us about the next phase of the operation. We would proceed as far as Sá da Bandeira, taking Fort Roçades and other towns on the way. However, at Fort Roçades another battle group known as Charlie, and consisting mostly of armoured cars, would join Zulu Force.

Gert would carry on in Ovambo with his counter-insurgency operations, while Hans would round up all the SWAPO bases over the ground we had just covered. Evidently UNITA had been forthcoming with information about these bases and would, in fact, act as guides to lead our forces to SWAPO. Just for the record, Hans had very little success. According to him, SWAPO was probably forewarned by his UNITA guides, with the result that his operation turned out to be a lemon.

The briefing session was memorable for one incident. It was very hot and stuffy inside the room where we were addressed by the Brigadier who tended to jump from one operation and subject to another and back again without any apparent pattern or logical sequence. This carried on for several hours and we all got rather confused and some also got bored.

Delville solved the problem by falling asleep while sitting right in front of the Brigadier. He slept soundly throughout the briefing and at the end he woke up completely refreshed but also completely in the dark as to our next move. This, however, did not bother him unduly because he cheerfully left for his headquarters after asking Corky at what time and in which direction we were supposed to move. Where we were going was unimportant.

After celebrating our first major success with a bottle of wine or two at Zulu headquarters, we turned in for the night.

The next day we would lead again, but this time with two troops of armoured cars. Connie's hairy assignment at the head of the column in a soft-skinned, lightly armed, clapped-out Land Rover had come to an end and none too soon, because he surely could not have lasted out the war as the permanent scout of Bravo Group.

SEVEN
Attack on Sá da Bandeira

We did not get off too early the next day because of logistical problems. The echelon had now been expanded with several more fuel tankers, both diesel and petrol, to cater for the armoured cars.

I now had an additional net to cope with, an armoured car net, which brought the total to three. Luckily the Zulu command net was rarely used because we were mostly out of range with Corky and his headquarters.

We passed the airfield, with C-130s already parked there, and headed for Mongua, the next town of any consequence. Later on I would become thoroughly acquainted with that part of Angola, but at the time it seemed to me to be mostly very dry bush, dry chanas and omurambas interspersed with miserable little kraals and small herds of thin cattle. We were deep into October and the rains had not yet come. Later on I would see the same bare dry area, with its brittle and dead-looking bush, become water-logged, green and lush into which even Unimogs would sink right up to their axles. Movement in the rainy season was restricted to the few all-weather roads, like the one to Mongua, Roçades and beyond, which was tarred all the way to Luanda.

We sped along, one troop of armoured cars leading, followed by myself in the Land Cruiser, a platoon of infantry, then the second troop and the rest of the column. It was relaxing and even peaceful to drive along without always expecting a burst of unfriendly bullets to find one's unprotected hide. This time the armoured cars would get it first, but with their armour protection around them they would have a far better chance of survival.

Mongua came and went quickly. It was, after all, only a small village with six or seven buildings.

Roçades, our next stop, was fast approaching when I was informed by Zulu headquarters that the town had already been taken by battle group Charlie.

Late that afternoon we cruised into the town and made our way to the fort situated on top of high ground overlooking the very long bridge spanning the Cunene River.

We took position along the eastern edge of the area just in front of the fort. I went to Zulu headquarters where I met Toon, the commander of Charlie, and some of his officers.

Toon is a giant of a man with flaming red hair and beard – a real rough diamond. He is an excellent fighting soldier. He was also the only man I had ever seen "putting on" an Eland-60, like putting on a pair of pants, instead of getting into it like other people do. His size made it impossible for him to ride in an Eland-90 because of the space taken up by the big 90 mm gun, thus his fondness of the Eland-60 as a command car.

I also met Aparicio and his ELP. Aparicio was a small, ex-Portuguese commander who, after their war, tried to join my old unit. He could, however, not pass the selection course and threw in the towel after about two days with me.

He left the army and formed ELP with which, according to him, he was going to liberate Portugal. ELP consisted of about 20 white Portuguese, all dressed in camouflage, hung with hand grenades and with machine-gun belts. Most of their G3 rifles had no stocks, an old Portuguese commando custom which meant that the rifle could not be fired from the shoulder. They normally sprayed their targets and much of the surrounding area by firing their stockless G3s from the hip.

ELP, and Aparicio, looked picturesque in their getup with the typical Portuguese fort as a backdrop. Any moment one expected to see Warner Brothers starting to shoot the usual war film full of heroics and camouflaged figures dashing through smoke and fire, teeth clenched in determination, eyes narrowed into cruel slits with stuttering machine guns clenched in capable fists.

Zulu Force was getting weirder and weirder as the war progressed. Aparicio was not exactly bubbling over with joy when he met me. After all, I had sacked him from the army as being unsuitable. He informed me that ELP would start their liberation of Portugal by starting in the south – Angola – working their way northwards through Portuguese Guineau, Cape Verde islands, Madeira and finally Portugal itself. Alexander the Great would be put in the shade.

Part of battle group Charlie had been to Peu-Peu up the river to capture this reported FAPLA stronghold where, according to the Brigadier, hundreds of military vehicles would be captured to ease our transport problem.

They returned before last light with nothing to show for their efforts. There were no vehicles, no weapons, no fuel, in fact no FAPLA. The place was totally deserted. The vehicles we had would have to serve us for the rest of the campaign, unless, with luck, we could liberate some elsewhere.

Meanwhile João had decided to move into town for a few drinks in what, I presumed, was the Portuguese equivalent of the local pub.

While standing at the counter, beer in hand, three FAPLA troops walked in, also intent on having a beer after a long day's hot patrolling in the bush. They were completely unaware of the fact that during their absence the town had been taken over by us.

They were therefore surprised and indignant when João, without further ado, gunned down two of them with his AK 47 and wounded the third who legged it to the fort at the top of the hill, intent on putting a complaint to his commander at FAPLA headquarters.

In due course this fellow turned up at the entrance gate to the fort where he was confronted by white South African sentries. The fellow was obviously agitated and because they could not understand a word of his Portuguese, they directed him in sign language to where my troops were laagered for the night.

I awoke to screams of laughter close by and, highly irritated, I got out of my sleeping bag to quieten my rowdy troops.

I found them standing in a circle having fun with a forlorn-looking troop in the centre. I gathered that he was complaining about being shot at by a stranger. Would the comrades come with him so that they could go and sort out the fellow in the pub downtown? Also, his mates were probably dead by now. The laughter increased and slowly the penny dropped.

"Are you FAPLA, comrade?" he asked one of my men.

"No, we are not FAPLA."

"What are you then?"

"FNLA!" The troops crawled with laughter.

The last I saw of the poor FAPLA troop was when he was led away under escort to Zulu headquarters, probably to be attended to by the doctor and the interrogators.

The next day we left Roçades, later to become known as Xangongo, and made for Humbe. Delville was leading with most of the armoured car squadron attached to him. Progress was fast. Humbe had already been taken by Charlie the previous day as they came up on the west bank of the Cunene from Calueque in the south. We passed Cahama, with no sign of FAPLA, and got to Tchibemba.

Here the forces were split the next morning. Delville had to move to Chiange, through to Jau and on to Huíla before meeting up with the rest of us at Rotunda.

I had to push on to João de Almeida and from there on to Rotunda. The armoured cars were split between the two battle groups, myself with the squadron headquarters and three troops and Delville with the other two troops.

The terrain was changing again as we moved northwards, becoming more broken, and in the distance mountains could be seen on the northern horizon. We passed through small villages and townships and arrived at João de Almeida in the late afternoon.

A fight broke out between the advance patrols and some FAPLA around the railway station. This station was quickly captured and I took Jack's company to capture the town itself with the support of the armoured cars and a group of four 81-mm mortars.

Oupa deployed his three inches with the 81s and sat there looking enviously at the beautiful equipment the 81s had. The 81s were manned by white South African troops and Oupa felt that he was beginning to lose his business to a more up to date crowd.

However, the mortars were not required and Jack's company concentrated in the vicinity of the Dutch Reformed Church, this being the heart of the country settled by the old "Dorsland Trekkers" from South Africa.

We found several stores full of rations, clothing and some ammunition at the railway station. This came in very handy, especially the rations, as we were more or less forced to live off the land. We also captured two lorry loads of what we thought was Angolan beer. It turned out to be ersatz wine, so sour that not even our troops would drink it. Shortly after midday we pulled out of João de Almeida and headed north into the hills, ideal terrain for fighting a delaying attack if FAPLA was so minded.

They were so minded and not long after leaving the town we ran into the first delaying position.

The terrain was thick, the going through the hills was tough and the road wound ever upwards to the top of the plateau. The armoured cars could not deploy off the road and we were basically reduced to fighting on a two-armoured car front.

Fingers came into his own with his machine guns mounted on the two Land Rovers. They could put down a heavy and sustained rate of fire and, at the short ranges we were compelled to fight, were more effective than even the armoured cars.

The leading platoon deployed rapidly, and under cover of the armoured cars and the Vickers machine guns, swept through the FAPLA position, killing many but not stopping to do a body count as time was precious.

So we swept upwards through the hills, being forced to fight three times before we could get clear of FAPLA's grip on our advance northwards.

At one time we overran one of the famous 122 mm rocket launchers, the first we had ever seen. This was a single tube, portable and accompanied by quite a number of rockets in boxes. We also killed the first Cubans in this area, probably crew members of the launcher.

At first I did not know what the weapon was that we had captured, until some of my FNLA commandantes got very excited when they saw the tube. They explained to me what it was. It looked very flimsy and I could not recall that the FAPLA troops actually took us under fire with it; evaluating its effect had to wait until a later date.

FAPLA must have suffered numerous casualties, because for weeks afterwards convoys moving through these same hills remarked on the almost continuous stench of decaying bodies between João de Almeida and Rotunda. We took no casualties, I think mainly because we brought down a very high concentration of fire very rapidly on the FAPLA positions, followed by a rapid assault by the leading infantry before FAPLA could recover from the shock.

We reached Rotunda by sundown. A quick assault on the high ground beyond secured the crossroads and also provided us with defensible terrain for the night. This assault was led by Charlie Company and they went through in grand style, although resistance was light.

I laagered on top of the high ground and Zulu headquarters pulled into the centre. The Vickers machine guns were dismounted, allocated to companies and the armoured cars distributed all along the perimeter, adding their weight of fire to the infantry. After all, we were only 20 kilometres from Sá da Bandeira and a night attack could be expected from that quarter.

Later on Delville arrived and he extended our laager to the south.

I made my headquarters on the stoep of a darkened and very quiet little house just to the left of the main road and thankfully went to sleep, feeling dead tired after three skirmishes and two company-sized attacks during the day.

Silence settled over the whole laager until I was woken by one of my troops. They had heard FAPLA moving in the bottom of the next valley and they were expecting an attack.

I heard nothing but ordered a stand to all the same, which was unnecessary since all my troops were already standing to, anxiously peering into the darkness.

Just when I thought it was a false alarm, FAPLA opened up with tracer from the high ground to the north and from the valley in-between. Vehicles started coming towards us, lights burning, which gave the 90 mm armoured cars some excellent targets to shoot at. Soon two vehicles were burning on the opposite slopes.

The Vickers machine guns meanwhile stuttered away, our mortars joined in and after a while the FAPLA attack died down completely.

One of my troops was hit in the head and they evacuated him to my headquarters where he lay groaning through most of the night, despite hefty injections of painkillers.

I was forced to move my sleeping bag to the yard behind the house, because the man's groaning kept me awake. Here I was met by the growling of an Alsatian housed in a kennel. He soon stopped, however, when I refused to budge. I spread out my sleeping bag and soon fell asleep.

In the early hours I was awoken by an almighty bang. Somewhat disorientated, I jumped out of my bag and went to a 90 mm armoured car blazing away at a vehicle on the opposite slope trying to sneak away to the north. Finally the vehicle was hit and a new funeral pyre was added to the previous two.

I went back to my bed and slept the sleep of the very tired but also satisfied that FAPLA was unable to dislodge us from Rotunda.

Next morning the sun awoke me and I made friends with the dog still in his kennel. We found a tap in the garden to wash and shave. The troop wounded in the head the previous night had died towards morning and his body was lying on the stoep, covered with a blanket.

We spotted some tentative movement inside the house, which we thought was deserted. The corner of a curtain was lifted and eyes peered anxiously out at us. The people must have been reassured, because slowly and carefully the front door was opened and the lady of the house appeared with a cup of very milky and very sweet coffee which she gave me. Frankly, mine, which I had just brewed, tasted much better. I did not refuse and to reassure the family swallowed the horrible syrupy stuff anyway.

Built into the side of the house was a small shop and I asked the Portuguese owner to open it as my troops would like to obtain some cigarettes. He obliged readily and the troops queued up, each clutching some escudos to pay for their cigarettes. The owner beamed because up to that time he had thought that I wanted the shop opened so that we could loot it.

When we left, we were the heroes and he and his family were confirmed FNLA supporters, especially when he saw the pile of escudos filling the till.

Corky briefed us about the attack on Sá da Bandeira which had to be delivered that day.

I was to attack the airfield on the south-eastern side of the town, secure it and not to proceed any further towards the city centre. Corky was fearful that my troops would get out of hand and that Sá da Bandeira would be sacked from end to end.

Delville was to approach Monte Christo, a high mountain that looms over Sá da Bandeira from the south, in a roundabout way and assault the crest up the southern slopes. Monte Christo was the dominating terrain and possession of the mountain would secure the whole of Sá da Bandeira. Stiff resistance was therefore expected during Delville's assault.

The next day Delville would come down the mountain with his troops and attack and clear the rest of the city while we would attack and secure the old Portuguese quartel area on the north-eastern side of town.

Sá da Bandeira, now known as Lubango, is a very large town by Angolan standards, the main commercial centre of southern Angola and the capital of Huíla Province. It is beautifully situated in a valley surrounded by mountains to the south, west and north. The streets are well laid out and, at the time, the buildings were substantial and well maintained. One also found parks, fountains, lanes of trees and numerous flowering shrubs to beautify the place.

We approached Sá da Bandeira along the main road coming in from the south-east with Monte Christo on our left. Somewhere to the south, but out of sight, Delville's Bushmen were preparing for a night attack up the steep slopes to take the summit.

Robbie had been detailed by me to take the airfield with his platoon and a troop of armoured cars. While he was doing this, the rest of Bravo Group had to wait on the road, as the airfield also dominated this one and only approach into the town. I therefore gave Robbie 15 minutes to complete his task, fully expecting that the real fighting would start as we entered the outskirts of Sá da Bandeira.

Robbie was to take the airfield by what one could term a *coup de main*. The armoured cars were to storm the airport terminal and take it under fire with the 90 mms while the infantry were to de-bus almost on the doorstep, storm inside the building, clear it and make particularly sure that they had the control tower in their grip. Any pockets of resistance outside the building would be mopped up afterwards.

Robbie understood his mission and he and his armoured cars left in a cloud of dust while the rest of us followed more slowly.

I was watching Robbie from a distance as he deployed according to plan. There was flame and smoke belching out of the terminal building as the armoured cars thumped away with the 90 mm guns. Little figures dismounted and stormed into the wreckage. Bursts of automatic fire could be heard.

Then one by one the armoured cars moved onto the airfield itself. The target was not the building any more but obviously some positions on the airfield beyond. I could also make out a line of infantry rapidly moving across to the nearest edge of the field with their rifles blazing.

After Robbie's 15 minutes had expired, it became obvious to me that there was more resistance there than we had bargained for. I could not reach him on the radio, so I moved forward to investigate.

When my Land Cruiser crossed the boundary fence, we came under small-arms fire from different parts of the airport.

The armoured cars were sitting on the apron in front of the wrecked terminal building, happily hurling 90 mm shells in all directions.

Robbie came running past with his platoon, heading for the eastern side. As he passed me, I could see that he was grinning from ear to ear. He had discarded his Russian helmet and was now wearing a cowboy hat which he had looted somewhere, probably in Roçades.

"No problem!" was about the only English he could get out under the circumstances when I enquired after his health. He did not want reinforcements, so I decided to leave Robbie to get on with it.

It was, however, fascinating to watch him while he was clearing the airfield. There were several positions all around the airport and Robbie dealt with each in turn. After some fire from the armoured cars, he would storm a position with his platoon with great spirit, rifles spitting away, with lots of shouting and swearing and finally emerge triumphantly on the other side.

Without stopping, Robbie would make for the next position at the double and go through the same procedure. Every time he passed me he would grin, give the thumbs-up sign and shout "No problem, no problem!" Obviously Robbie was enjoying himself tremendously.

Slowly, FAPLA prisoners were gathering at the traffic circle where the road to the airport turned off from the main road. The fire slowly died down and finally Robbie and his tired crew also slowed down to a walk and then at last stopped completely. The airport was theirs.

We had few casualties: only one man, a white Portuguese, seriously wounded in the chest and the rest were lightly wounded. FAPLA bodies, however, were strewn all over the airfield and the approaches to the terminal building. We counted over 80 bodies and we estimated that there must have been a battalion dug in all around the perimeter. The *coup de main* obviously caught them off balance.

We also took about 30 FAPLA prisoners. Among them was one who was not more than ten years old. When he saw my

Land Cruiser he ran forward, fell on his knees and started pleading for his life. I understood from him that he had been press-ganged into service by FAPLA, that his father was FNLA and that he was in jail in Moçâmedes, which is also where his mother lived. I appointed him as my batman and he joined Paul and myself in the Land Cruiser. His name was João, so I called him Junior as there were already too many Joãos in my organisation.

The prisoners were passed on to Dries eventually and we proceeded to launch our attack against the eastern suburb of Sá da Bandeira.

I attacked with Jack and Connie's companies, keeping Costa's company in reserve. Three troops of armoured cars were giving support, as were my three-inch mortars. Delville had the 81 mm mortars to support his assault on Monte Christo so that their fire was not available to Bravo Group.

The assault went through rather rapidly, resistance being light, and it became obvious that the main resistance had been centred around the airfield where we had managed to break FAPLA's back.

A car came up from the city, however, heading for the airport, and it came face to face with an armoured car which had its 90 mm pointing down its throat. The car swiftly turned around to flee but was stopped by machine-gun fire.

At the scene we found the black driver killed behind the wheel and two dead white Portuguese on the back seat, one male and one female. A very dazed and slightly wounded Portuguese was sitting by the roadside. The armoured car commander felt very bad because these were obviously civilians who happened to stray into a combat zone at the wrong time. The wounded Portuguese was taken to the Shell filling station which we used as a collection point for casualties, prisoners and other non-combatants who strayed into the area.

After a while our advance stopped on our final exploitation line. Across a valley to the north we could see dozens of vehicles, heavily loaded with troops streaming out of the quartel and heading to the north-east, away from town.

Toon moved the armoured cars as far forward as he could, the river at the bottom of the valley being an obstacle, and opened fire on the quartel at maximum range. I wished that we had the 81 mm mortars with their superior range so that we could create havoc among the fleeing columns.

The cars tried their best and some of the shots did fall inside the quartel. This only sped up the evacuation by FAPLA. We certainly could see no evidence of serious damage to the buildings. We thought it was rather unsporting of FAPLA to leave without even offering a token resistance.

Meanwhile Delville had also reached his objective at the top of Monte Christo, finding little resistance. They settled down around the magnificent statue of Christ, a replica of the one at Rio de Janeiro, to watch me and my men scurrying around like little ants at the foot of the mountain. They later reported that it was a magnificent view and that they appreciated our warlike displays put on for their special entertainment. They also complimented us on our faultless drills which appeared just perfect, viewed from their lofty perch above the scene of battle.

We gave up shooting at the rapidly disappearing FAPLA because they were getting out of range, and consolidated our position for the night.

The captured Portuguese civilian came to me with a request that I should give him a free pass to emigrate to Brazil. He was sick and tired of Angola. He gave his name as D'Oliviera and told me that he was a school teacher in town. I therefore gave him permission to go home to his family, but he refused, saying that FNLA would kill him.

A little way off a FNLA soldier stood listening to the conversation, obviously conversant with English. When he understood that I was on the point of sending D'Oliviera home, he came across immediately and protested vigorously. According to him, D'Oliviera was a very high-ranking officer in FAPLA.

And so it turned out to be. Under Dries's skilful interrogation he admitted that he was, in fact, in charge of MPLA's propaganda machine, that he had come to Sá da Bandeira from Benguela to motivate the local FAPLA as they were in a state of panic after our initial successes. Our rapid advance towards the city filled them with a feeling of doom, and panic was beginning to spread through the FAPLA army.

The male white Portuguese killed in the car was a military advisor to the FAPLA military commander of the whole area, which included Huíla Province and Benguela. He came along to help plan the defence of Sá da Bandeira and was also the pilot of a light plane which was parked on the apron at the airfield when our attack went in. It was, in fact, the sounds of battle that caused them to break off in the middle of a conference in order to head for the airfield to make good their escape.

They were not quick enough, however, and the airport was already in our hands when they came face to face with our armoured car.

The Portuguese lady turned out to be the FAPLA commander's wife. She too was an important person in the MPLA hierarchy.

Our armoured car commander felt much better when I gave him the details of his unexpected "bags". So did FNLA when D'Oliviera was finally handed over to their political hierarchy as a prisoner.

As I was out of radio touch with them, I drove back to Zulu headquarters, still at Rotunda, to inform them of our success. I wanted to make a full report to the ops staff and also re-establish radio contact with Willie on the radio. On the way there, I managed to make contact with Willie on the radio.

"I am on my own." I could almost hear the sigh of relief over the intervening distance of several kilometres.

At Rotunda I put Corky in the picture and he moved his headquarters to the terminal buildings on the airfield. He was not too happy with the way we had treated the building. All the glass was shot out, electricity and water installations wrecked, furniture and fittings were in splinters, there were large ventilation holes in brick walls and the whole building had a generally wrecked appearance. Coupled with this, there were bodies lying around everywhere, which would shortly begin to add a rather "pongy" contribution to the general atmosphere of warlike desolation and wreckage.

Corky got some men to collect the dead and to bury them in a mass grave, but for many days afterwards many more would be discovered lying in long grass, the stench of rotting bodies giving them away.

Corky's headquarters was, in fact, not a very salubrious place to visit. It stank to high heaven. They probably got used to it eventually. I never did and I usually stayed for as short a time as possible. Corky probably felt that I was ill-mannered, but it was difficult to tell him that his headquarters "stank".

We also captured a fine selection of beautiful serviceable aircraft, only a few of them shot up by Robbie's escapades. One was the aircraft in which the FAPLA commander, his wife and D'Oliviera arrived. In its cargo we found a brand-new AK-47, a submachine gun, a pistol and lots of very interesting documents which kept Dries happily busy for quite a few days.

There was also at least one Aztec and a Queen Air in beautiful condition. The others were single-engine light planes, all in flying condition. All belonged to MPLA and therefore were legitimate war loot. It was not very long before a ferry pilot arrived to fly them out one by one.

The next morning we went for the quartel, advancing in copybook style in long extended lines and supported by the armoured cars and Oupa's mortars. Oupa had to move his mortars by bounds, as usual, and was hard pressed to keep up with the advance.

Finally, when he was in range, I allowed him to fire a few shots into the quartel, mostly to see if we would get any reaction. There was none.

The armoured cars moved to the four corners of the high wall surrounding the building from where they could support us, if necessary, and also cut off any FAPLA trying to escape.

The infantry poured through the impressive main gate and entered the long three-storey main building, clearing rooms as they went.

A troop of armoured cars stormed through the centre arch under the main building onto the parade square beyond, and deployed ready to fire on anything that moved and looked like FAPLA.

We found a couple of confused old gentlemen, with hard hats and brown overalls, floating around aimlessly. They informed us that nobody was in camp when they pitched up for work that morning. They, in fact, were a couple of labourers who just turned up for work at the normal time, as they did for the Portuguese Artillery regiment stationed there once upon a time, as they did for the FAPLA more recently, and as they would do for FNLA in the immediate future.

Some people have the ability to see wars come and go, to adapt to whichever situation comes their way, to let fate roll over them without offering resistance and to consider their way of life to be completely normal. Maybe it is. Maybe we are the abnormal buggers who always strive to change situations and people to suit us, not always for the better.

We also found huge hangar-like stores, bordering the parade ground, crammed with weapons, ammunition, camouflage fatigues and rations.

This was a windfall, especially for the white troops manning the armoured cars, as their only issue was a pair of trousers and one shirt. Over the next few days everybody – Bushman, FNLA, white South African – was completely re-issued with brand-new combat fatigues.

We checked out the main building and while there was a lot of rubbish lying around, indicating a hasty departure, it was comfortable and convenient enough to act as Bravo Group headquarters and accommodation for the officers. Paul, Junior and I moved into the large plushly furnished office of the FAPLA commander with its heavy oak desk, deep armchairs, deep carpets and heavy but empty bookcases lining the walls. It was on the second floor overlooking the parade ground. Headquarters was established in very stylish surroundings. We also found a pub downstairs, which became the officers' club.

The troops moved into comfortable but empty bungalows behind the headquarters, the vehicles were put in the vehicle park and the armoured car squadron "tiffies" opened up a very effective little workshop in the already existing facility. Our vehicles could be seen to at last.

Meanwhile Delville's troops had come down from their mountain and cleared the central city area. No resistance whatsoever was encountered.

In front of the quartel was a large tarred plain with an island in the middle. After the quartel had been taken, an armoured car was parked there with its 90 mm gun pointed down the road leading into town.

It was just about 0800 hours, time for men to arrive at their places of work all over the world.

I had just joined the armoured car to chat to the commander when a civilian car, painted drab olive, approached us from the direction of town. It stopped about two paces from me and the armoured car.

The car was driven by a soldier in camouflaged fatigues. In the back sat two gentlemen, also in fatigues, one with a splendid red cap on his head.

I was completely flabbergasted for a moment and then the penny dropped. They were FAPLA! And they were armed.

So I unslung my rifle and let fly with a couple of bursts into the back of the car. Driver and occupants were taken by complete surprise, but I suppose reflex action on the driver's part took charge and he took off in a cloud of dust nearly running me over, made a U-turn and sped away in the opposite direction back to town. The armoured car opened up with its 30 mm Browning and I revved them with my rifle, but the car had almost disappeared around a corner before we managed to force it to stop.

We followed up quickly in the armoured car, but found only the dead driver behind the wheel. One passenger had been badly hit, or was killed, but was dragged away by the other passenger.

A day or so later a badly wounded civilian was admitted to hospital. He turned out to be the fellow with the red cap, deputy commander of FAPLA in the area, and he was on his way to work when he was so rudely brought down to earth by us, right in front of his own headquarters.

It did not seem possible that after the previous day's assault on the airfield, and the morning's attack on the quartel, that there could still be people in Sá da Bandeira who had any doubts about the identity of the troops driving around the place with armoured cars while flying FNLA flags and yelling FNLA slogans.

Maybe the FAPLA deputy commander came from out of town that morning and maybe he thought that we were Cubans who had come to help them in stopping the advance of the hated "Boers".

EIGHT
Moçâmedes

The Brigadier flew in during the day, all smiles at our success and particularly at the incredible rate of advance since the campaign started about two weeks earlier.

All systems were "go" and we were briefed to take Moçâmedes in order to open up a port for logistical support.

A similar force to Zulu, but named Foxbat, was meanwhile poking its head out of Nova Lisboa on the major highway to Luanda. It consisted mostly of UNITA troops and a squadron of armoured cars. Eddie was the commander and he had with him such well-known characters as Hollie and Nic, both paratroopers and both friends of mine.

There would therefore be two thrusts towards Luanda: ours along the coast to open up the ports as we went, and Eddie's somewhat further inland on the main route to the north.

We were not quite sure how far north we were supposed to go because nobody really told us. Some among us thought that we would try to capture as much of Angola as possible before 11 November, the official date of independence for Angola, in order to make UNITA's position viable and strong enough to at least counteract the communist-supported MPLA.

Others thought that our intention was to capture the Benguela railway, thus cutting the export routes of troublesome neighbours such as Zambia.

Still others thought that we would go for Luanda in order to put Dr Savimbi firmly in the Angolan saddle.

My own FNLA troops, of course, asked similar questions and got somewhat different answers. As far as they were concerned, the war aims of FNLA had been achieved. Somewhere along the line either Chipenda or Kombuta had informed them that the aim was to take Sá da Bandeira, probably because they thought that this was all we were capable of. With Sá da Bandeira in hand, the surrounding area would be built up into an FNLA bastion and the troops would be discharged to settle and make a living in this newly created FNLA heaven.

The result was a deep-running feeling of dissatisfaction and resentment when it became clear to my troops that the war was a long way from over and that they were required to march once more, maybe all the way to Luanda.

So one morning I assembled the whole battalion to try and explain to them why we could not stop now, but had to defeat FAPLA before peace would come to Angola.

They stood in their ranks, in their companies, a sullen mass of troops who just needed a small spark to openly start a mutiny.

I had prudently warned a troop of armoured cars to stand by, because I had no intention of having myself and my fellow South Africans killed by a mob of unruly Angolan FNLA soldiers.

So I started my speech, in English, but translated by Paul. Immediately there was uproar as some of the instigators began to shout and agitate the crowd. Things were getting out of hand, so I signalled the armoured cars to take up positions, one on each corner of the parade ground with their 90 mm guns trained inwards. The shouting died down to a murmur and finally ceased.

When everything was deadly quiet, some little FNLA chap in the front rank started up again, shouting and shaking his fist, trying to inflame those around him.

I lost my temper, stalked into the ranks, grabbed him by the chest and pulled him out where I proceeded to box his ears in no uncertain manner. He finally sank to his knees and asked me to stop.

Welcome sounds of laughter from the crowd was my reward, so I settled down to tell them once again what the war was all about. I was getting their attention and the four armoured cars helped to emphasise the points I was making.

Just as I was approaching the high point of my speech, driving home the fact that we were fighting for the survival of a free

Angola, free from communism or imperialism, an awful racket broke out on the parade ground behind the last ranks of the battalion.

A stupid clot of a "tiffie" had "liberated" a motorcycle and had decided to fix it up in the workshop. At that moment when my speech was reaching its climax, he decided to take it on a trial run on the parade ground, completely oblivious of the parade in progress and of the importance of the occasion.

The bike was exceedingly noisy, so that my hard-hitting, and I thought, catching phrases were completely drowned.

"Anton! Shoot that bugger's bike! Now!"

I had a platoon leader by that name standing nearby, so with some alacrity he went into action.

He cornered the cyclist and must have looked extremely dangerous coming at the offender at the double with his FN rifle at the ready. The "tiffie" abandoned his motorbike in a hurry, leaving it lying on the ground with wheels spinning and engine roaring.

Bang! Bang! Bang! Anton fired three shots into the offending motorbike's engine and the noise died down. The bike would never pound the streets of Sá da Bandeira again. From around the corner a white-faced and shocked "tiffie" stared at the demise of his motorcycle, their short-lived partnership having come to an abrupt and violent end.

A deathly hush settled over the troops. To them it was now quite clear that the old man was exceedingly angry, and with 90 mms turned inwards, it could be their turn next.

I finished my speech, the high notes successfully destroyed by the "tiffie", but seemingly it did not matter. The troops had made up their minds. It would be better to go along with this mad South African than thwart him.

It was obvious, however, that the troops had to be kept busy and that I had to get rid of the undermining elements, mostly former FNLA commandantes who had lost their prestige among the men, having been forced to take a back seat after the South Africans took over the command slots.

ELP came to my rescue. Aparicio had decided to put the first steps of his grand scheme in motion. He would declare a free republic in Huíla Province with himself and his men as the ruling junta.

Some of my FNLA came to me, very disturbed naturally with the news that Aparicio had declared over the local radio station that they were the new chiefs in "Indian" country. Until then I did not even know that there was a radio station.

I therefore informed Corky that Aparicio was creating problems in Huíla Province by grabbing the fruits from FNLA's efforts. ELP had taken no part in any fighting at all and were conspicuous because of the distance they placed between themselves and wherever some fighting was going on.

Corky did not see as big a threat in Aparicio's actions as I did, but he also distrusted him. He admonished Aparicio about the contents of his radio transmissions which should have been intended to calm the people, not to win support for him and his organisation. Corky also informed him that Shylock would now act as "mayor" of the town and that all decisions regarding the disposal of loot and captured booty would rest with him.

I got João and the other commandantes together and informed them that FNLA was in danger of losing Huíla Province. I therefore suggested that they should form some sort of a political committee, wrest control of the broadcasting station from Aparicio and his ELP and start their own broadcasts.

It suited them perfectly and soon they moved out of the quartel into no doubt more luxurious quarters in town where they established themselves as an FNLA governing body. Aparicio and crew soon had to give up any pretentions to a position of power in southern Angola.

To keep the troops busy I sent Jack and his company to Hoque, on Corky's instructions, on the main road to Nova Lisboa to clear away all FAPLA as far as the town. He took two troops of armoured cars with him.

There was no evidence of FAPLA until they reached Hoque itself where they ran into a well-laid ambush. Jack told me he had never seen troops dismount so rapidly as his did, sliding down from the mountain of kit stacked in the backs of their trucks.

A fierce battle developed with the armoured cars joining in with their machine guns. They were too close to the enemy positions to use main armament. Jack finally overrode the FAPLA positions and proceeded to clear out the town of Hoque. FAPLA suffered heavy casualties, Jack only a few, and it was altogether a very satisfying action.

They came back to the quartel late that night full of war stories and ready for our nightly cold beer, paös and cheese in our rather comfortable officer's club.

Connie was sent to Vila de Arriaga, down the escarpment to the west and along the old road to Moçâmedes. I went with him.

We passed through some spectacular scenery as the road wound steeply down the side of a very rugged mountain range, almost an exact copy of the Drakensberg, although not quite as high.

The rainy season had started and streams were beginning to tumble down the mountainside into the thickly vegetated foothills below. Further to the west one could see that the landscape was getting flatter and progressively drier towards the Atlantic coast.

We arrived at de Arriaga, a neat little village at the bottom of the pass and found only a few officials manning the railway line. There was no sign of FAPLA, so we returned to Sá da Bandeira.

Costa and his company I sent back to João de Almeida as, by all accounts, some gangs of FAPLA who we either bypassed, or who re-formed, were floating around in that area, threatening our lines of communication.

They stayed for about a week and during that time accounted for about 150 FAPLA.

We had captured two 82 mm B10 recoilless guns, very useful in both the anti-tank and anti-personnel role, and these we mounted in two Land Rovers.

We also managed to squeeze six paratroopers out of Corky who received a whole platoon of them but kept most for protecting his headquarters. I split the six into two teams of three for each of the B10s and they proceeded to train under Connie's direction to fire these guns. At last I had a viable anti-tank capability within Bravo Group, discounting of course the 90 mm armoured cars which were not really part of Bravo.

We were now ordered to Moçâmedes. Delville was moving with Zulu headquarters down the escarpment on the new tarred road to Moçâmedes and Bravo was taking the road via Vila de Arriaga.

Our move to de Arriaga was rapid, as we had covered the route before. Beyond de Arriaga we entered one narrow defile after another, flanked by high hills quite close to the road and therefore ideal ambush positions. As a precaution we were cutting the telegraph line every few miles.

Just as the terrain began to flatten out, we ran into some FAPLA resistance. Evidently a small patrol had set themselves up in a delaying position, probably when they saw the head of the column appearing through the mouth of the valley to the east. They could not have had any idea of our actual strength, because they ended up being pulverised by the advance patrols of armoured cars, an infantry platoon and Oupa's mortars. We killed five of them, including one female FAPLA soldier, the first we had seen. The rest disappeared into the bush at great speed.

The little skirmish was memorable only for the slow deployment of Mecchie's platoon. Mecchie, so called because he used to be an air mechanic, was taken to task by me and informed that they would lead the advance henceforth until I was satisfied that his platoon's reaction was sharp enough.

To lead the advance of a column is not the healthiest position to be in. As a result, Mecchie's platoon got sharper and sharper during each contact, at the completion of which all would look at me with expectation in their eyes. But I hardened my heart and I kept them at it until some days later, long after Moçâmedes was taken, I moved them to the rear and replaced them with another platoon which, strangely enough, also acted with alacrity every time we struck a contact. The lesson must have spread throughout the unit.

The winding road and the caution with which we moved made us late in arriving at Karakula, the centre of Karakul farming in Angola. Here we rejoined the main road to discover that

Delville had long since passed through on his way to Moçâmedes.

The terrain here is very similar to the Karoo as it is closer to the coast and the arid desert strip, which is a continuation of the Namib Desert further south.

So we drove on westwards into the gathering gloom until we were finally stopped by Corky's headquarters and told to pull off the road.

Ahead there was a fierce battle ranging. Delville had run into a strong FAPLA position and tracers were streaming across the night sky. Every now and again we could see the flash of an explosion followed by the deep crump of a mortar.

Silhouetted against the sky we could see the old vehicle on top of a sand dune. The terrain had, by now, changed to pure desert and the whole battle had a very Second-World-War-Western-Desert atmosphere about it. With a bit of imagination one could almost see the Eighth Army and the Afrika Korps slugging it out among the dunes.

We laagered, as our predecessors did in the Western Desert, in long lines of vehicles. We set out our defences as they did and we brewed our tea and cooked our food on burning tins half filled with sand and petrol, as they did.

With tracer, flares and crumping mortar shells in the background the Western Desert picture was complete. Even the chill that set in.

We got up the following morning in a desolate landscape. The fighting had long since stopped and ahead were the sand dunes where FAPLA had tried to stop Delville.

Bravo was to pass through Delville's Bushmen, to advance to Moçâmedes and to take it. Corky had another very nice air photograph of the place, which assisted me in planning the attack through the town.

The town had a similar layout to Pereira de Eça except that it was much bigger.

I decided to attack with both companies, one to the east and the other to the west of the long main street. We would have one section, supported by one armoured car, for each street running parallel to the main street. The cross-streets would be used for co-ordination lines.

Jack's company, however, had to clear the approaches to the town first in order to secure a start line for the final assault.

Oupa's mortars and the 81s would give fire support on call, with the three inches, as usual, being forced to move in bounds to stay within range. The machine guns would move on the eastern flank to give support where necessary. I would control the assault line and rate of advance.

Afterwards Jack was to clear the old airfield to the east and the new one to the south-east. Connie was to take his company to Porto Alexandre, a fishing harbour down the coast and to secure it for us.

Corky gave me a guide in the form of a local Portuguese who had pitched up at his headquarters the previous night. His name was Martins (pronounced "Martiens").

Corky had also given a Portuguese parachute unit residence in Moçâmedes, with an ultimatum to pull out if they did not want to get involved in the battle. The previous day a small liaison team from the Portuguese Army had come out to make contact and to assure us of their neutrality.

There was a Portuguese naval frigate in harbour and because Corky feared intervention from the ship in favour of the MPLA, he instructed the naval officer who accompanied the senior army officer to have the ship out of the harbour by first light. This was done. The paratroopers still in town were later flown out to Luanda with Corky's permission.

We took over the advance from Delville, passing the signs of the previous night's battle while doing so. Wrecked and burnt-out vehicles were cluttering the road, with some still smouldering bodies, called "smokies" by Delville, lying here and there. Delville had captured quite a bit of material also, among others another 122 mm rocket launcher but this time mounted in a brand-new Unimog.

As we approached the only bit of vegetation in the whole area, this time a dense forest through which the road passed, we came under small-arms fire. So from a sand dune situation we moved into a jungle situation, clearing the forest in next to no time with our infantry. Mecchie was leading, going into action like greased lightning.

We then crossed the combined road and railway bridge over a dry riverbed and entered the town proper.

Jack cleared the approaches and two companies formed on the first lateral road we came to, each section with an armoured car in attendance.

The long line of infantry, followed by the armoured cars, moved forward in copybook style. There was no sign of life anywhere, the population keeping indoors and being no doubt somewhat apprehensive that FNLA might take it into their heads to start looting, killing and raping. It must have been a pleasant surprise to see them moving through under strict control, well disciplined and at least looking like professionals.

Inside the town we found no resistance, but we struck quite a strong pocket as we left town on the southern side. A very sharp firefight developed between Jack's company and the armoured cars on one side and FAPLA who were dug in around the FAPLA headquarters. This lasted for probably 30 minutes after which FAPLA withdrew in the direction of the airport.

We captured a large quantity of equipment at the headquarters in the form of numerous weapons, including excellent hunting rifles, ammunition, rations and large quantities of the most expensive brandies, liqueurs and whisky. Needless to say, the latter was strictly guarded, but Jack, later on in a moment of mental aberration, loaded it on an Air Force C-130 to be shipped back to Rundu for our consumption at a later stage. This was the last we saw of our Napoleon brandy and our Glenfiddich whisky.

Jack moved his company to the old airport where, after a short skirmish, the rest of FAPLA were either killed or captured.

Connie moved into the dockyard area against no resistance and a veritable treasure trove was exposed to our incredulous eyes. There were dozens of brand-new tip trucks, about 400 brand new pickup vans, dozens of tractors and bulldozers and all sorts of other equipment filling the warehouses. Many of the vehicles and earth-moving equipment were destined for Zambia but, because of the war, never got there.

Connie then went on to Porto Alexandre, which he took without resistance. He was back at Moçâmedes late the same evening.

The town was secured so I took Martins, who was sitting in the back of my vehicle, to the one and only decent hotel in town. By this time people had turned out into the streets and we were passing through one cheering throng after another, especially when they recognised Martins.

Martins could not restrain himself and he was returning the cheers with his hands clasped above his head, the conquering hero. Every now and then he gave the FNLA sign.

"Martins! Martins! Martins!" the multitude screamed and a simple trip to the hotel became a triumphant procession for Martins, with the crowds falling in behind us and trotting to keep up with the Land Cruiser.

I dropped Martins off at the hotel where he was promptly mobbed by a back-slapping, kissing and hugging crowd and I broke clear in the direction of the esplanade and the old fort.

No doubt Martins became the next mayor of Moçâmedes.

Moçâmedes was quite a clean and attractive place, especially the esplanade overlooked by the old Portuguese fort where I found the Angolan Police unconcernedly going about their business. I made my number with the Chief of Police and had some coffee with him. We parted on friendly terms.

The harbour is a very large natural one, with general cargo jetties on the southern side and iron ore jetties around the bay, on the northern side. The latter were newly built and could handle the biggest bulk ore carriers.

There were also some fish and crayfish factories beyond the main dock area with a number of deep-sea trawlers moored offshore to keep the factories supplied.

With its railway stretching to the interior as far as Serpa Pinto, Moçâmedes was therefore quite an important port and simplified our logistical system.

We assembled near the old airport where there was a magnificent skeet shooting range, to await the Brigadier who would arrive the next day.

Junior meanwhile traced his mother and younger brother and brought them to our laager. Like a real professional he showed Little Junior, who was four years old and a miniature edition of Junior, around the armoured cars and guns. Little Junior thought Big Junior was a hero and as they wandered through the parked armoured cars, hand in hand, the adulation in Little Junior's eyes for his brother was obvious.

I arranged with Junior's mother that she should take him back – much to his disgust, because he wanted to be a real fighting soldier. We loaded her with rations and blankets. Junior and family departed happily and father was released from the Moçâmedes jail in due course.

The Brigadier arrived in fine fettle. The war was turning out to be a pushover and the advance was far more rapid than expected. Together with brigade headquarters, the Brigadier inspected the Portuguese paratrooper quartel which was left by them in a frightful mess. Human excrement on tables, beds and chairs was a common sight. Ration packs lay everywhere. The latter could be used, however, as we have always found Portuguese rations to be rather good, better than South African ration packs anyway. Not that we could get our hands on any South African ration packs at the time.

We also sent for Charlie Company. They were to stay behind as occupying force and to ferret out any pockets of FAPLA resistance. The population obviously were very pro-FNLA as we were, for the moment anyway, the winners. In Africa one always backs the winner and one does so enthusiastically in order to remain in a healthy condition for as long as possible.

Needless to say, Costa and Silva with their ex-DGS experience and their intimate knowledge of both Portuguese and African Angolans soon secured the area after our return to Sá da Bandeira.

NINE
Joining up with Frank

Back in Sá da Bandeira we found another FNLA force, under command of Major Frank, ensconced mostly in a block of flats, south of our artillery quartel.

They consisted of two companies formed and trained by Frank and other South Africans in Serpa Pinto. I was surprised to meet up with them as I was completely unaware of this additional FNLA force, even though I must have passed through Serpa Pinto while Frank was knocking shape into his troops.

Because Chipenda had his headquarters in Serpa Pinto, Frank saw him fairly frequently and he could enlighten me on our "boss's" drinking and womanising habits which, by all accounts, were of no mean proportions. He was evidently also a great orator and motivator and could sway his audience with seemingly very little visible effort.

Corky decided that instead of forming another battle group, Frank's two companies should form part of my Bravo Group and that Frank should become my second in command.

So Grobbie and Jock came across to us with their FNLA and became Charlie and Delta companies respectively. Costa's old Charlie Company, still in Moçâmedes, became an independent company.

The two new companies looked good, well equipped, with a smattering of Zaire-trained FNLA commandos among them. They wore distinguishing red scarves to indicate that they were graduates of the commando school. Prominent among them was Commandante Geraldo, who was Frank's right-hand man in dealing with black soldiers. Frank also wore a scarf and he looked quite natty in his new camouflage uniform.

I also found some members from my old unit among the platoon leaders and was very happy to see them.

Unfortunately, Nic, whom I had asked for to become my second in command had been waylaid by the Brigadier while on his way to Bravo Group, and he was sent to join UNITA in Nova Lisboa. We could have used Nic's organising capability and his sense of humour. Frank, however, turned out to be a star in the field of organising so that, in the end, I really only missed Nic's hilarious jokes and his personal friendship. Nic and I had come through many years in I Parachute Battalion and later on he become my second in command of a specialist unit.

The day after our arrival back in Sá da Bandeira I was sitting on my haunches on the back verandah of the main building, boiling water in my "fire bucket" over a small fire fed with Pimlico box planks, when an apparition stopped next to me with an arrogant "Bon Dias" (good day).

I looked up and saw this splendidly dressed individual in crackling new camouflage fatigues, shining boots, red scarf and a length of red mountain rope, complete with two interlocking karabiners, around his rather fat stomach. He had gold braid on his shoulders, wore a peaked cap and sunglasses. Behind him was another equally well-dressed individual, but less gaudily adorned, carrying the first apparition's briefcase.

The man was obviously very high ranking and, judging by the scarf and mountain rope, considering himself to be a graduate of the commando school in Zaire.

Luckily Paul was sitting nearby, waiting for his tea. He was quite useless in preparing food or drinks and therefore happy to have his commanding officer do it for him. Paul therefore translated.

"I want to speak to the FNLA commander!" said this fellow rather brusquely.

"I am the FNLA commander." I retorted. "Who are you?"

"I am General (I forgot his name) and the newly appointed military governor of Huíla Province. I would like to speak to the black FNLA commander, not to you!"

I eased myself back on my backside. "There is no black FNLA commander. I am the only commander of the battalion, so you will have to speak to me."

"In that case I would prefer to speak to the company commanders."

"You do not speak to the commanders on their own, but I am willing to call them so that you can say what you want to say to all of us."

I got Paul to fetch the company commanders. I proceeded making my tea, offered some to him out of my huge fire-blackened and unhygienic-looking "fire bucket" but he, rather impolitely I thought, declined. He did not move, but let his eyes roam over the parade ground, the barracks, the armoured cars and piles of captured weapons and equipment. Finally my company commanders rolled up and he was shocked.

"But I thought they were black? What has happened to the Commandantes? Why do you only have white officers?"

"Well, I sacked the Commandantes because they were bloody useless and the troops don't like them anyway. All they did before we came along was to hang back in the fights and exploit the men to their own advantage," I replied.

"Can I speak to the troops then?"

"No, if you have something to say, say it to me and I will carry it over to the troops."

"In that case I am wasting my time. Good day." He stalked out indignantly, followed by his equally indignant minion carrying his briefcase.

I could not be sure, but because of the barely avoided near mutiny I had to cope with earlier in a rather high-handed fashion, I suspected that he was making a renewed bid for the loyalty, and services, of my troops so that he could have a strong military tool at his personal command to enforce his authority in the province.

That was probably the reason why he came to the quartel unannounced, but at the same time making a grand entrance, hoping to throw the South Africans off balance, thus getting the opportunity to speak to the troops knowing, of course, that we would not be able to understand one word of his address.

Later that evening we were briefed by Corky. The advance was to resume the next morning with Bravo Group leading.

I never found out whether Corky knew about the "General" in his fancy outfit. I certainly did not deem it necessary, or important enough, to inform Zulu headquarters and for a while the "General" moved off the stage to surface again, much later in the campaign, in somewhat less conspicuous circumstances.

Mortar attack on enemy position near Pereira de Eça.

Members of 32 Battalion checking out an abandoned hut during patrol.

Collecting identity documents after a successful encounter with SWAPO insurgents.

Some of the Russian rifles and Cuban webbing found on dead SWAPO members.

A victim of 32 Battalion sprawled in the grass after a short and fierce encounter. The victors move on.

Destroyed petrol pump, Pereria de Eça.

Impromptu conference with UNITA, southern Angola. Johnny Katale on the right.

One of the many abandoned small towns in southern Angola. A lone soldier strolls down the main street of Quito early evening.

Pereira de Eça took a hammering during the fighting. An old man waits patiently for transport to the south.

Following heavy fighting in the area, most Portuguese decided to move out – like this convoy, watched by youngsters.

A farewell handshake to South African troops from a resident of Pereira de Eça, before moving out.

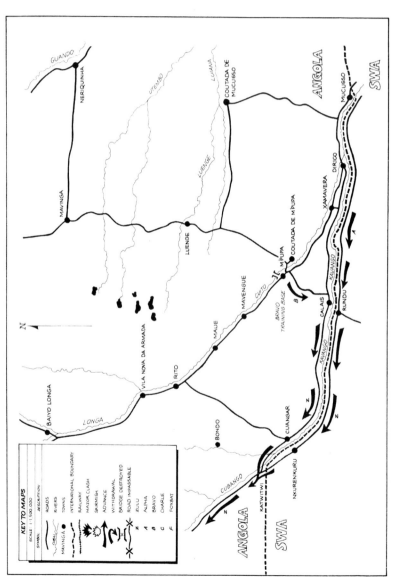

Battle group Alpha and Bravo concentrate at Rundu to form Zulu Force and commence the advance into Angola.

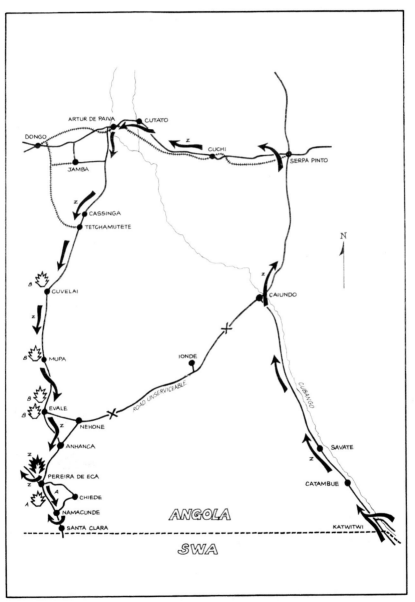

Advance of Zulu Force via Serpa Pinto and Artur de Paiva to Pereira de Eça.

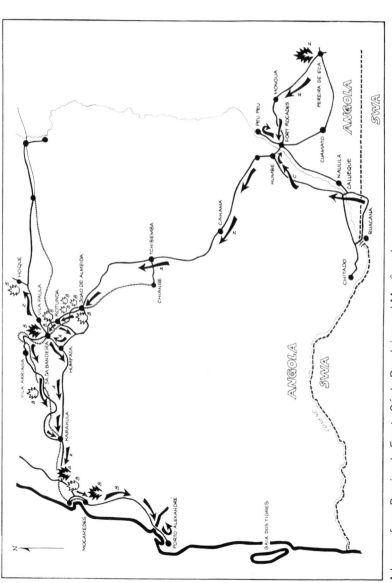

Advance from Pereira de Eça to Sá da Bandeira and Moçâmedes.

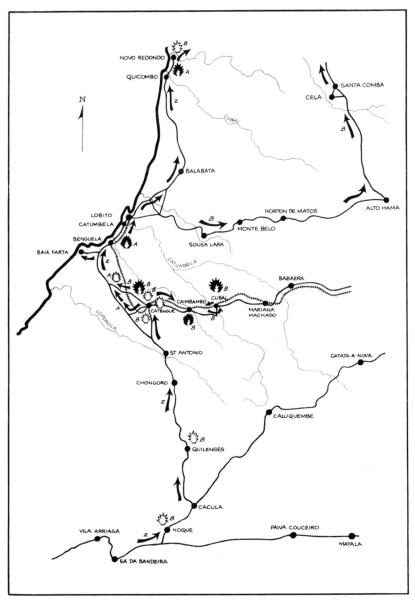

Advance from Sá da Bandeira via Benguela to Novo Redondo. Bravo switches to the central front around Santa Comba.

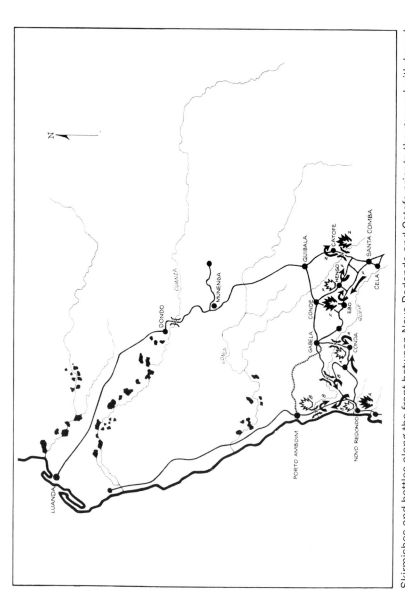

Skirmishes and battles along the front between Novo Redondo and Catofe prior to the general withdrawal of all South African, FNLA and UNITA forces.

TEN

Catengue

We were glad to get away from Sá da Bandeira with its undercurrents of manoeuvring for influence among the various factions. On our last day UNITA also entered the fray, which left the city a steaming and boiling cauldron of intrigue.

Bravo had to leave one company behind: Delta Company under Jock, to be used by whomever took over from Corky as commander of peacekeeping troops in the city. This left me, once more, with three rifle companies and the mortar and machine-gun platoons. The anti-tank platoon quietly died as most of its members elected to stay behind in Sá da Bandeira, finding politics more to their liking than fighting, especially against Cubans.

Jack led through Hoque, where he had his previous brush with FAPLA, and turned left towards Catengue. There was no sign of FAPLA until we reached the next fairly large town.

According to Dries, and our forward patrols, there was a FAPLA presence there, so the leading armoured car troop took up position and started to shell the most likely and suspicious-looking areas in the town.

Jack shook his troops out into two assault platoons. With one in reserve and with one platoon on each side of the main street, he started to clear the houses.

There was no resistance. Unfortunately, one civilian was wounded by a shell from one of the armoured cars as he ran in a panic from the area of the service station to the cover of the bush on the outskirts. No doubt the sudden appearance of the cars and the subsequent shelling was too much for his nerves, already severely strained by previous fighting in the area between FAPLA and FNLA.

Luckily he was not badly wounded. Our doctor soon stitched him up and we could send him home in reasonable shape.

We spent the night here and Delville took over, running with the ball the next morning.

While the Bushmen were advancing steadily up the road, my troops spread themselves out rather leisurely on the shady stoeps, out of the scorching sun, while waiting for my order to board their vehicles.

Unfortunately, Corky decided to drive through the town, for some reason or other, and he was not impressed with the Bravo "mob" lolling about in all attitudes of lazy repose without taking the slightest notice of their Brigade Commander.

It was a rather putout Corky who found me at the town entrance. He was more than a little angry. "Your troops have no discipline," he began in the strictest tone of voice he could muster, which for Corky was not all that easy.

This put me on the defensive, as only I was allowed to call my troops useless or ill disciplined. "I don't believe you. They are even better disciplined than the white troops or the Bushmen," I said, conveniently forgetting about the near mutiny a few days ago.

"Why do you call them ill disciplined?" I continued.

"They refused to respect me, to get up off their backsides, and I even have problems getting into your camp. They treat their Brigade Commander with a certain amount of disdain!"

"Corky, I don't believe it. They always come to attention and salute when they see a senior officer."

"Well, let's drive through town and I will show you how your troops lounge about. They are even too lazy to chase away the flies."

So Corky and I got into his vehicle and we drove down the main street. As far as we went, groups of soldiers smartly jumped to attention, saluted and grinned from ear to ear. I glanced at Corky. He was furious.

"You must teach your troops to pay their respects to me also and not only to you and your officers. Tell them who I am, dammit. You have never informed them that I am the higher commander."

Later during the morning a gentleman from a café across the road came strolling over to make our acquaintance.

To my surprise he kicked off in perfect Afrikaans introducing himself as Mr Visser. I pretended that I did not understand him, but he was blunt in informing me that the whites in my force were South Africans because he could recognise a South African, particularly an Afrikaner a mile off. After all, he was descended from the Dorsland Trekkers and a Boer can recognise another Boer anywhere in the world.

According to him, FAPLA had left the previous day and were waiting for us at a bridge further up the road. Evidently, we had arrived just in time for him because FAPLA was about to close his café, the only one in town. I left him to Dries who proceeded to milk him dry of all relevant and irrelevant information, this being the job of an intelligence officer.

Finally we mounted our vehicles and followed on behind Delville. He meanwhile had reached the bridge but, due to information given to us by Mr Visser, had decided to outflank the FAPLA positions dominating the bridge from the high ground beyond and to cross the river lower down. We had to wait for Delville to resolve the situation one way or another. He had had a few skirmishes on the way and it was logical to expect FAPLA to cover the bridge and so delay our crossing.

The positions on the north bank looked tremendously strong. There was, however, no visible sign of FAPLA, which did not mean much as they were good at concealing themselves and even their crew-served weapons.

The hours ticked by and finally Corky could contain his patience no longer. He ordered the armoured cars to get into firing positions on the hill overlooking the bridge and to blast the visible newly dug positions on the other side. This was done for approximately ten minutes without reaction. Corky and Dries then led on foot followed and covered by armoured cars. Since no sign of life was present and no fire was drawn, an engineer protected by a patrol inspected the bridge.

Demolition charges were found, but the charges were very poorly laid. Even though FAPLA tried to detonate them, their ignition system was defective.

The FAPLA on the other side probably left the scene the moment Delville's leading armoured cars appeared from the south.

By this time Zulu Force's reputation for unexpectedly fast movement and violent action was preceding us in no uncertain fashion and I think many a FAPLA commander had his job cut out to keep his men in position the moment they heard that we were on our way. Mostly the commanders were unsuccessful and they probably did not try very hard as they themselves were not too keen to face the irresistible advance of Zulu.

Corky gave the ball back to us while Delville was trying to extricate his battalion from the difficult terrain he unexpectedly found himself in while trying his outflanking manoeuvre.

We rapidly advanced to a farm just short of Catengue where we laagered for the night.

Delville came in with his men long after dark, thoroughly cheesed off with the river, the swamps, the terrain in general and some of his Portuguese leaders.

I pushed out a patrol about a kilometre up the road towards Catengue consisting of a troop of armoured cars, a platoon of infantry and two B-10s, manned by the paratroopers from 1 Parachute Battalion.

Just before last light a FAPLA patrol came sneaking up the road, probably to probe our position and strength, and they ran straight into my security patrol. A brisk firefight developed to which we were interested spectators since we were laagering on high ground overlooking the scene of action.

Too soon the entertainment stopped and we went back to cooking our meals. FAPLA scarpered back up the road towards Catengue and as far as we could make out there were no casualties on their side. We certainly had none, but I prudently redeployed the security patrol further forward, towards the enemy, in case they were going to have another go with a stronger force.

The farmer quite happily supplied us with goats, which we paid for in looted Angolan currency. It certainly was a change to indulge in the good old South African custom of a "braaivleis", even if the meat was goat's meat.

At first light we kicked off the advance with Connie's company leading, fully expecting a full-blooded fight in Catengue itself.

Catengue straddles the main road from Benguela to Nova Lisboa in the east and Sá da Bandeira in the south. It is also a very important station on the Benguela railway line. The road from Sá da Bandeira forms a T-junction with the Benguela–Nova Lisboa road and by taking Catengue, we would be behind the right flank of the FAPLA forces facing UNITA further to the east.

Catengue was therefore extremely important to both sides.

Very cautiously we approached the town from the south. The mortars were deployed and most of the armoured cars were as far forward as possible to bring to bear their firepower. Connie's company was stretched out in extended line to clear the town.

Nothing happened and there was an eerie silence over the whole place. Suddenly a sedan appeared from the direction of Nova Lisboa and it was promptly brought to a fiery standstill by one of the armoured cars. On closer inspection, the occupants appeared to be senior officers from FRELIMO, the Mozambique resistance movement, who were with FAPLA in the field as "observers". The war was getting more international by the day.

Their "observing" came to an abrupt, unexpected and violent end in Catengue. We were quite cheerful about our "catch". Their obviously high ranks made up for the lack of numbers.

Connie moved through the village and pronounced it clear of any FAPLA, even of civilians who had completely absconded. This was the first town in which we found no civilians. This looked rather ominous. We had no idea where FAPLA could be.

I informed Corky that the place was cleared and he moved in to establish his headquarters under a huge baobab tree, on the bank of a dry stream bed.

During the proceedings there was a huge thump to the west, a cloud of dust, followed by the sighting of a missile passing over our heads and exploding behind us with a tremendous bang and black smoke.

It was a 122 mm rocket, Katyusha or Red Eye as they became known later on in the campaign.

I did not know what to make of this, as only one rocket was fired.

Rather perplexed, I decided to send Jack's company in that direction, on the main road to Benguela, for a distance of about five kilometres, in order to clear the hills and approaches to the west.

Connie was sent towards Nova Lisboa, also for about five kilometres, on a similar errand.

Both had to take up blocking positions to protect us and Zulu headquarters while further cunning plans were made by Corky and his staff to proceed with the war.

Toon and myself sat under the baobab, each with a cup of tea, brewed by Zulu headquarters, while contemplating our higher headquarters in action.

Willie, Corky, Dries and others were busy with a sand model for a briefing session when all hell broke loose in Jack's direction.

Toon and I looked at each other and we both decided that Jack could handle it while we had our tea.

The crescendo of battle increased alarmingly and seemed to be coming in our direction. It could only mean that Jack was coming back, and in a hurry, which would be rather awkward for our Zulu headquarters, happily engaged on their splendid sand model, oblivious to the world around them.

So we finished our tea and proceeded to the scene of battle, Toon in his armoured car and I in what suddenly seemed a very open Land Cruiser.

I found some of Jack's company on the outskirts of the town, rapidly putting distance between themselves and FAPLA. Most did not even want to stop and talk to me. They probably did not even recognise me, their own commander. With difficulty I rallied a few and turned them around again towards the enemy.

Jack, the remains of his company, and a troop of armoured cars were about four to five kilometres up the road.

The only problem was that not far outside town mortar shell

bursts were mushrooming continuously up and down the tar road, and the only way to get to Jack quickly was to run this gauntlet, whether one liked it or not.

Paul and I therefore charged the mushrooming clouds at top speed.

Shells fell all around us, the odd one even on the road. The noise was tremendous and I was told later that at one point the Land Cruiser disappeared completely under the impact of a near miss.

We reached the armoured cars where they were in position behind a crest, pounding away at FAPLA about 800 metres further up the road.

Just below us, and slightly behind, in a cutting were the four 81 mm mortars, firing at a very rapid rate of fire and also very wildly. As I watched, one of the mortars had a cook-off, the barrel being extremely hot and the shell fell about 200 metres ahead of us. The mortars were also under fire at the time and almost simultaneously, with the cook-off, the discarded secondary charges caught fire and flared up with an intense flame and smoke. Mortarmen ran in all directions.

For a moment I thought that I had lost my 81 mm mortars, but when the smoke cleared they were still there with the mortarmen moving back rather apprehensively to continue firing. It was obvious, however, that there was no fire plan as all shots were scattered widely over the FAPLA positions.

My poor old three-inch mortars were champing at the bit, but I could not deploy them as they had insufficient range to reach the FAPLA positions. Rather incongruously, therefore, they were deployed in depth, behind the 81s, mainly to be there as a secure base of fire in case FAPLA forced us back further to the outskirts of town.

Ahead of the armoured cars was a low rise, about halfway to the FAPLA positions. Beyond that was the river with its bridge and just beyond that I could see the main FAPLA positions.

I saw no trenches but could see a lot of back blast and smoke in their positions as they were laying into us with recoilless guns, 75 mms and B-10s. Also, there were a lot of heavy machine guns just in front of the crest, creating quite a respectable curtain of fire through which any advance would be suicidal.

At the foot of the FAPLA hill could be heard a continuous crackle of automatic fire. This perturbed me greatly as I was under the impression that Jack and his men were still in an eyeball to eyeball confrontation with FAPLA along the west bank of the river. I was therefore most upset with the armoured cars who appeared to have left Jack's company in a very dangerous situation while they belted it back for cover out of immediate danger from the recoilless guns.

I thumped on the troop leader's hatch as I was getting somewhat angry and very apprehensive about the safety – even survival – of Bravo Company.

"Why did you leave Captain Jack and his men while you ran for the nearest cover? You should have brought the infantry back with you or stayed with them to fight it out."

The troop leader had his hatch open only a wee crack as he had no intention of getting clobbered by flying shrapnel.

"But sir, they came back with us," he replied.

"Where are their lorries then?"

"They abandoned them just short of the bridge."

The troop leader himself was now getting apprehensive because if I was unable to find Jack, then he and his company probably skedaddled all the way back to the town, maybe even beyond, which meant that the armoured cars were now without infantry support.

The enemy mortars were intense and every now and again a salvo of about four or five Red Eye rockets would arrive. We later discovered that the enemy had in fact deployed fifteen 82 mm mortars and a battery of Red Eye rocket launchers mounted on vehicles.

Without significantly reducing their volume of fire, my own 81s were now shooting at the base of the FAPLA positions from where the light automatic fire was coming.

Soon they had run out of ammunition and their commander reported accordingly. At no time did I notice a mobile fire controller, who could have controlled their fire much more effectively. All the ammunition they fired was consequently wasted. They just added to the general din of battle and that was all that could be said for them.

Somewhat disgusted I acceded to the mortar commander's request to take his mortars out of action.

Meanwhile I had spotted Jack through the thick bush, slightly right of the armoured cars. I made my way across and saw what was probably all that was left of his company: not more than 40 or 50 men. Some of those I turned at the town were coming up from the rear, so the company was slowly getting back to a reasonable size again.

Jack had a few serious casualties and quite a number of fairly light ones. We did not know how many were killed or missing. Even Nel's face was covered in blood from a shrapnel wound in his nose, which made him sound like a man with a severe attack of adenoids.

Jack told me that he had dismounted in front of the bridge and that he had spread out to go through the dry river in extended line. On the other side FAPLA suddenly opened up with very heavy automatic fire at very short range and Jack's advance just faltered, broke down and turned into an uncontrolled "retreat".

Jack had a hell of a job on his hands to stop his men in their present positions. The company still looked very jittery to me, but at least they were obeying commands to stay where they were and not to scamper for the rear. Just the smallest spark, however, would no doubt encourage them to continue their head-over-heels rush for safer abodes further to the south.

There was no doubt about it. We were facing the best organised and heaviest FAPLA opposition to date and we just had to win this one or the Bravo troops would never fight again. The situation called for a tangible sign that their commander was not worried about the outcome. I most certainly was not at all confident that we could stop FAPLA before they had overrun Corky's headquarters. A bit of play-acting was called for.

I therefore started to collect firewood, knocked up a fire and started to brew tea in the company's position.

Here and there troops began to smile when they saw me obviously preparing to stay for a while. The "old man" was not contemplating a hasty retreat. The position could not be too bad therefore, and slowly the company started to fight back.

Meanwhile I had been on the radio to Zulu headquarters with the request that the services of a full 81 mm mortar platoon, freshly arrived from Sá da Bandeira that morning, be made available.

I also wanted my machine-gun platoon to move up to give us more firepower from the crest of the hill we were sitting on.

Also Grobbie's Charlie Company was to be ready to move if they should be required.

Toon brought up another two armoured car troops so that with them and my Vickers machine guns we were beginning to look quite respectable. FAPLA in any case had now missed the boat if they intended to push us out of Catengue.

After a while a little fellow with a radio set turned up at my command post, which I had shifted to higher ground on the left of the cutting. He introduced himself as the new mortar platoon leader and asked me where he should establish his base plate positions.

Shells were falling all around our position, but he was completely unconcerned. It was a most remarkable performance as this must have been the first time in his military career that he was under fire, and the fire was far too intense for a comfortable introduction to war.

After consulting with him it was decided to deploy them more or less with the three-inch mortars, about 1000 metres to the rear.

He then proceeded to discuss his fire plan with me, which was a refreshing change as the previous mortar commander forgot all about fire plans. I thought that the crew-served weapons on the crest of the FAPLA hill should be put out of action with some concentrated mortar fire. Afterwards we could tackle the FAPLA positions at the foot of the hill.

He listened respectfully but then suggested that he should use his mortars in a counter-bombardment role first, since the enemy were really plastering us with theirs, and then go on to the other targets. In other words, my plan was not too clever. The platoon leader's calm self-assurance was astonishing. It would be rare indeed in one's military career to see mortars used in the counter-bombardment role. One needed equipment such as the cymbeline to give an accurate range and bearing to the enemy mortar positions. The heavier artillery, which we did not have, are normally used in a counter-bombardment role, certainly not mortars.

"How would you do it?" I asked.

"Well, sir, I can hear their mortar tubes every time they fire. I will take a bearing on the sound of the first one firing, press my stopwatch, wait for the shell burst from the salvo, press it again, get time of flight, adjust roughly for the speed of sound, look at my 81 mm mortar range tables opposite the adjusted time of flight and get a rough range. I then adjust for my own mortar positions, give them a bearing and range and play my mortars up and down, 400 metres either side, of the calculated enemy base plates."

This youngster, about 5'6" tall, thin and insignificant in looks, had worked out very calmly a rough-and-ready counter-bombardment system while under very heavy enemy mortar and rocket fire.

"Jump to it," I said with enthusiasm because we were taking quite a few casualties. It was not very pleasant being plastered by enemy shells.

He did his calculations and soon all eight of his 81s were barking back at the enemy's fifteen 82s. After playing his mortar fire up and down as he had intended, the enemy mortar fire slackened considerably and even stopped as they bounded back to get out of range of our 81s. They started up again later but could not reach us effectively from their new positions.

All we had to contend with were the recoilless guns, their heavy machine guns and some Red Eyes.

In front of me three paratroopers were virtually sitting in the open with their B-10, firing away at each and every flash on the FAPLA side and silencing some as well.

My machine-gun platoon was getting into action against the FAPLA at the foot of the hill from positions spread out along our crest. Soon the incredible sustained fire of the 12 Vickers guns, sweeping from side to side across FAPLA, forced their automatic weapons to shut up.

The armoured cars were doing their thing by belting the crest of the FAPLA hill, and especially the highest point in the area of the road cutting, with 90 mm.

They were, however, running out of ammunition and had to withdraw troop by troop to replenish again. This was the first time that our cars had had to replenish during an action so that my black troops were completely unaware of their replenishment drills.

When therefore the first troop, the one that gave Jack his initial support, scarpered to the rear with guns traversed rearwards towards the enemy, Jack's company thought it was a withdrawal and decided that they had to accompany them. Jack and I had our jobs cut out to get his men back into position.

All in all, things were beginning to look up. Zulu headquarters was safe and the time had come to think about driving FAPLA off their position.

I made a request to Corky that Delville's troops make a left flanking attack on FAPLA's position while we supported him with fire from the next crest about 400 metres in front of us.

Corky came back with a counter-proposal that Delville should take his whole battle group on a march around FAPLA's right flank to a position some miles behind them where he could take up ambush positions while we would drive FAPLA off the crest, towards Delville, with my Bravo Group.

At first I was a bit dubious, but after consulting the map, I could only but agree to Corky's brilliant plan.

So I asked for Charlie Company to come up on our right while I shifted Jack's Bravo Company to the left of the cutting.

I shouted to Jack to come to an order group at my command post. As he jumped up and ran to the rear to get behind the crest before crossing the road, the company jumped up with him and followed him.

A swearing Jack, using his boot with great abandon, finally convinced them that he was not leaving them in the lurch but that he was only going to have a few words with me. They slunk back to their positions slowly and rather shamefaced and continued to return the FAPLA fire.

An order group was held with Toon, the two company commanders, two mortar platoon leaders and the machine-gun platoon leader attending.

We were still under fire, but from my position we had a good view, so we stayed where we were.

The plan was to go for the first crest initially with the cars supporting us while the mortars and machine guns would spray the FAPLA slope. After taking the first crest we would pause, wait for the cars to come up, and take up firing positions on the intermediate objective. We would then go for the final objective, the FAPLA hill, while all support weapons would give fire support, even the three inches which could then be moved to base plate positions within range of the objective.

Oupa's eyes lit up, because so far he had been missing the action.

With our Vickers machine guns, the two mortar platoons, the three armoured car troops and our one B-10, I thought we could swamp FAPLA on their hill.

Unfortunately, I did not consider the continuous light automatic fire at the base of the hill to be significant.

Frank and James, newly arrived with Grobbie and his Charlie Company from Sá da Bandeira, joined me at the command post.

James would co-ordinate all supporting fires and the movement of the various support weapons groups.

Frank, as 2 I/C, would be ready to take over from me or to dash off to a critical part of the battle.

All formed part of my headquarters which would move on or near the Catengue–Benguela tar road, the axis of attack. Initially we would stay where we were, until the initial objective had been taken, then move forward with the cars to be on foot for the rest of the assault, roughly in the centre of the two companies.

The intermediate position was taken with no resistance from FAPLA and all support weapons redeployed while the infantry caught their breath and plucked up their courage for the nasty final assault.

This kicked off as planned, but soon Charlie Company, on the right, were lagging behind in the very rough and thick terrain.

Jack was making good progress on the left and I had to restrain him.

Bravo Command Group, walking on the road, was beginning to get small-arms fire from our rear.

Immediately my mind went back to a previous time when the old Charlie Company took Zulu headquarters under fire north of Evale.

"Grobbie, tell your depth platoon to stop shooting. They are shooting at us on the road," I called to Charlie on the radio.

Grobbie came back a short while later and informed me that his depth platoon was not shooting. It therefore had to be FAPLA. I was perplexed and frankly did not believe him. To my right, in the thick bush, there was a lot of shooting, and shouting, as we approached the river and the base of the high ground beyond.

We had passed Jack's abandoned trucks and, apart from flat wheels, they appeared to be in order.

Again we came under rather accurate small-arms fire and this time I sent James to tell Grobbie that his troops were clobbering us and that we were not FAPLA but on their side.

Five minutes later James was back with the information that Grobbie was having a rough time to crack through a line of FAPLA trenches in front of him, which we in the Command Group could not see because of the thickness of the terrain to our right.

One of Grobbie's troops came bursting out of the bush on our right, ran up to me and in broken Afrikaans said "I look for the hand grenade. There are a lot of enemy in a hole."

I gave him a grenade, having visions of a nice deep hole filled with FAPLA into which he wanted to drop a grenade, hopefully with devastating effect.

He, however, had run up against the FAPLA trench system and, quite rightly, thought that a grenade would be of great assistance, although he certainly underestimated the effect of one grenade on a well-prepared system.

Charlie Company finally broke through the FAPLA trenches and took the remainder of their part of the objective.

Jack had experienced no resistance whatsoever while occupying the dominating high ground on the left.

On the way up, we in the command group came across a number of recoilless guns and heavy machine guns with their crews, all of them Cubans, lying dead behind their weapons. Some crew-served weapons were just abandoned, as was the command post where the Cuban commander had left his maps and other documents while he hastily made tracks for the rear.

We also found the terminal ends and the electrical firing device for a demolition with the leads leading to the bridge. Following the leads we found that they had been cut, probably by a 90 mm shell during the initial contact earlier in the morning.

I arranged with Frank to consolidate our position, to move up our mortars, machine guns and armoured cars and to take up a position of all-round defence.

Meanwhile I would go back to Zulu headquarters to report and to change my damaged Land Cruiser for my second vehicle, a short wheel-base Land Rover we had captured in Moçâmedes.

While driving through a shell burst in the morning, my Land Cruiser had collected a few fragments in the radiator and water pump and it was now overheating. To get to my Land Cruiser, Paul and I had to walk back the way we had come, to the first objective. It was rather dicey because a lot of FAPLA were still around in the bushes alongside the road.

Corky and Willie at one stage came forward to see if I required assistance or whether Corky should take command of the situation and use the total force. Corky was rather concerned about the heavy enemy fire, the black troops' apparent unwillingness to go forward under fire and also the fact that my Land Cruiser had been hit. When I arrived back without incident, I could tell a rather relieved Corky that everything was in hand. The armoured car squadron light workshop troop took away my Land Cruiser for repairs.

I was still discussing the whole battle with Corky when renewed fighting broke out to the west on the FAPLA hill we had just taken. Frank was having a set-to with FAPLA and I could not raise him on my radio. Immediately Paul and I rushed back in the other vehicle.

Mortar fire could be heard and some automatic fire, but the mortar fire was definitely our own three inches and not FAPLA mortars.

We reached Frank where he was trying to get Charlie Company into the thick bush to assault FAPLA, which were still ensconced in part of the trench system, now behind and between us and Zulu headquarters.

For a while everything went well and Toon and I were beginning to relax, in the ex-Cuban command post, as the enemy fire began to die down and stop.

Charlie Company came back, struggling and crashing through the bush, and out of ammunition. Frank replenished Charlie Company from stocks carried by Bravo Company. Jack had not used any ammunition in the final assault, so he had plenty to spare.

Toon and I were still admiring the scenery and the Cuban maps, while Frank was getting on with his interrupted consolidation, when a fresh bout of automatic fire broke out, this time from very close quarters almost on top of the hill. We ducked down into the ditch as the fire swept over us. FAPLA was launching a counter-attack in force from their trench system in our rear. We were now in fact cut off from Zulu headquarters with a large FAPLA force between us and them.

With my rifle I did my best to return fire to an enemy estimated to be not more than ten to 15 paces from us and in thick cover.

Toon had nothing, not even a pistol, and his armoured car was parked in the cutting just below us. The ground between us and his car was swept with automatic fire, so that old Toon was pinned down with me and without means of returning fire. He was a very unhappy armour man reduced to the normal state of all infantry men in battle: hugging the bottom of a ditch or a hole while the enemy is trying very hard to get you with a variety of shells, bullets and so on.

"Commandant, lend me your rifle!" he pleaded desperately.

"Why?"

"Because they are shooting at us and I have no weapon!"

"You must be mad! This is my rifle!" I retorted.

There was no way I would give up my trusty weapon to an unarmed tank man when FAPLA was about 15 paces away.

Frank launched another assault, generally downhill, with the support of the three-inch mortars. They at least succeeded in pushing FAPLA away from our immediate vicinity so that we could at last raise our heads. Soon the assault ran out of steam. The troops were getting tired, but it was also getting late. We had to consolidate before last light, because the last thing I wanted on my hands was a confusing fight in thick bush after dark.

Charlie Company came back, looking crest-fallen, and Frank informed me that he had run out of ideas to get FAPLA off the hill.

I approached Toon to discuss using his armoured cars to support another assault. It was just an idea, using armoured cars, but I had to agree with Toon that they would not be able to move and shoot in the thick bush.

Meanwhile Fingers was looking at me with a hopeful and pleading expression.

"Frank, why don't you use Fingers and his machine guns. You can use them as LMGs to give close-fire support while Charlie has another crack at FAPLA."

Fingers beamed and started to get the Land Rover-mounted machine guns ready before we could change our minds. They were to be carried by the crews during the assault, to be put down on their tripods and to produce heavy sustained fire at short range while the infantry cleared out the various FAPLA pockets.

The mortars could not give support fire, because of the danger to our troops where the thick bush effectively cut down fighting distance between FAPLA and our troops to a matter of not more than ten paces.

The assault went in once more. This time it was splendid to hear the fighting move further and further down the hill, northwards along the foot of the hill, and finally dying down in the distance. The sustained slow bursts of the Vickers guns were too much for FAPLA.

As the light faded, tired but happy troops came staggering out of the bush, the sweating Vickers crews carrying the guns proudly on their backs. It was about 1800 hours when fighting finally ceased. The fight had lasted from 0900 to 1800 without any let-up whatsoever. For virtually the whole time, the fire from both sides was very heavy. It had been a very long day for all of us, including, no doubt, for FAPLA.

As was customary, and probably with many FAPLA still unaccounted for as they were floating around somewhere in the thick bush, we established an all-round defensive system. I posted a security patrol consisting of an infantry platoon, armoured cars, and the B-10 about one kilometre up the road towards Benguela.

The B-10, however, never left. It was some time after they were supposed to have moved out that two of the paratrooper crew members came to me and informed me that the third member had refused to go out with them and that he had now disappeared.

This was very disquieting. The paratrooper was, after all, a member from one of my old units, but it was pointless looking for him in the dark. I therefore resolved to deal with the matter the next morning.

Earlier in the afternoon Delville had a glorious turkey shoot as FAPLA, many of them Cubans, and mostly command elements drove into his well-laid ambush positions. Numerous vehicles and trucks were left burning as the fleeing enemy drove helter-skelter for Benguela as an unorganised mob, all control having broken down. It was during the night, after the fighting had died down on his front, that Delville was approached by a FAPLA soldier who informed him that there were several FAPLA comrades who would like to receive assistance from him and his men. He probably thought Delville was a Cuban and the fact that Delville spoke Portuguese reasonably well perhaps reinforced his slight miscalculation. Delville set up an RV and a time to meet up with the FAPLA soldier and his mates.

When the time arrived, the bird had flown. Maybe they heard from other fleeing troops of the havoc Delville and his troops were wreaking on the fleeing FAPLA forces.

We slept like logs, tired out after a very busy and violent day. The next morning we started to clear the battlefield, collecting 75 mm and B-10 guns, some 12,7 heavy machine guns and inspecting the trench system which stretched away north of the road for almost a kilometre in two zigzagging lines. Only then did we realise that we were, in fact, up against much more than a battle group of the enemy the previous day. All signs pointed to a full-blown regimental task force and we marvelled at our temerity to attack them with two companies supported by three troops of armoured cars, mortars and machine guns and at our luck at pulling it off.

Charlie Company, in fact, finally broke through on a front of not more than 200 metres in the very thick bush during their final assault on the objective. They were completely unaware of the fact that most of FAPLA was still left intact behind them when they got to the top of the hill.

FAPLA quickly reoccupied the trenches that we had cleared, which accounted for the fire my Command Group was getting from the rear during the assault, and also for the fact that we were subjected to determined FAPLA counter-attacks from our own rear, while Frank was still consolidating our positions.

I thanked my lucky stars that I had twice passed very closely to FAPLA troops without being caught or shot at, while they were reforming: once when going back on foot and the second time when coming back to the objective with my replacement vehicle. Imagine the consequences had I been captured!

Dries was very happy with the documents, and particularly the map we seized from the Cuban command post. It reinforced our opinion that we had been faced by a regiment-sized unit, probably one thousand men with all their support weapons.

The map also showed Zulu Force's advance, up to that date, and as it was projected into the future. Their intelligence was absolutely spot on, or so I was informed by Dries, as I had no pre-knowledge of our intended conduct of the war.

A young, blond, crestfallen paratrooper also reported to me. I was in a quandary and also angry because I had to deal with a clear case of cowardice in the face of the enemy.

But I also remembered seeing the same young man sitting in the open behind the sights of the B-10 the previous day. He was the number one of the crew, calmly plastering the enemy crew-served weapons for hours while mortar shells, rockets and other projectiles were exploding all around us. For him it must have been a very long day. It was his first time in action against an enemy where he had to face lead, and so much of it too.

"Sir, I am sorry I ran away last night. I was scared," he said, his face colouring red.

"Where did you go?"

"I slept under a bush in the laager."

"Paratroopers don't run away. Why did you? Are you not proud of being a paratrooper?"

"I know, sir. I am sorry. I won't do it again. Please give me another chance."

I gave him a second – and last – chance and the youngster left to join his crew. How he got past them I do not know, but I subsequently saw him always cool and calm in action, absolutely unflinching – or so it appeared. He was determined not to fail again and he never did.

I am glad I gave him another chance, and kept what happened to myself and the other two members of the crew.

ELEVEN
Courage and Cowardice

There is physical courage and there is moral courage. Those who are in the know claim that moral courage is a much rarer commodity than physical courage. If one is fortunate enough to be a morally courageous person, then physical courage is automatically added to one's arsenal of desirable qualities.

Let me reflect on both types of courage and its opposite, cowardice, also of two types. I have seen very brave people in action and, unfortunately, very cowardly people in the field of battle and also in the conference room. So one also has physical cowardice and moral cowardice.

How does one define physical courage and how does one measure it?

I have seen men without a shred of fear who become reckless under fire. They are the ones who will charge on enemy positions single-handedly, thinking nothing of it during the process, only being slightly surprised if they collect some metal on the way. They seem to be convinced that they are invincible, that enemy fire will not touch them.

These men have been known to do some foolish things, even needlessly getting their comrades killed, especially when they are in a position of command.

When the reckless charge comes off, one will, of course, collect the medals afterwards and this may serve as encouragement to further reckless charges in the future.

Then there is the man who feels fear inside him, his mouth having a dry coppery taste, his stomach feeling heavy and in great urge to discharge itself willy-nilly, the eyes being wide and staring, pulse rate up and all the fear symptoms manifested in a high-pitched, shaky voice. Sometimes one has to make several attempts to speak or to give an audible and intelligent command under conditions where there is a lot of incoming lead, all seemingly aimed at one person.

If one overcomes such a debilitating sense of fear and goes into action against the enemy in a seemingly cool and calm fashion, then one is doing what is expected of a soldier, to stand and fight instead of running away. Most soldiers I know can do this, being outwardly cool under fire although eaten by fear inside. One does not expect more than that from anyone. It is a happy day in any commander's life when all his subordinate troops act in this way, possibly only after intensive training and after they have been in some scraps with the enemy. They have become veterans and are, as veterans, extremely valuable, especially when pitched against a "rookie" enemy or, as in the case of Savannah, against an enemy not well known for their martial prowess under fire. (I think particularly of the Cubans who always left the battlefield first, in fact deserting their black FAPLA allies to our not-so-tender mercies.)

But to return to our fearful little soldier, under heavy enemy fire, who is struggling to keep cool and to do his duty as is expected of him. If now some crisis situation arises which must be attended to immediately in order to prevent a disaster, the same little soldier may be required to do something more than just staying cool under fire.

A machine gun may be pinning him and his comrades down in the open where they are taking casualties. An assault on the machine gun must be made in order to save themselves.

The courageous leader, while fear threatens to overcome him, will encourage his men to assault with him, pointing out that if they do not, they will all shortly be dead.

If they do not want to come with him, fear glueing them to the ground, he may muster enough courage to do the job on his own, thus saving himself and his men.

This is courage, overcoming fear that threatens to paralyse and because it is necessary, decisively acting against an unrelenting, persistent and extremely dangerous enemy.

But that kind of courage can also be unthinking, even if one is not in the same category as the reckless soldier. The sudden injection of adrenalin into the bloodstream when a crisis situation suddenly develops helps towards a very rapid and sometimes automatic reaction which, in the cold light of day, will appear as an act of bravery. The soldier concerned may truthfully say that he did not even have time to think before he acted.

It is the fellow who has time to think, who is not in a crisis situation, who must still carry out his task, and who must overcome dangerous and difficult circumstances, who possibly displays more courage than the soldier we discussed previously.

Consider the same small group of men moving into an attack and again getting pinned down by machine-gun fire but, this time, not in the open but behind adequate cover, which will make the possibility of casualties reasonably remote.

A task, however, had been given and unless the machine gun is overcome the objective cannot be reached. This is where a strong sense of duty may come into play.

If the leader now can encourage his men to jump up from behind relatively safe cover to follow him across an open space, with no cover and splattered with all sorts of nasty bits of enemy metal in order to take out a machine gun, then he is displaying courage of a very high order.

If his men refuse to budge from behind their comforting bits of cover and he is forced to do the charge through the open, then he is extremely courageous, although perhaps not such a good leader of men as one would like him to be.

The point is that the fellow has time to think, must suppress his fear and force himself to move from relative safety into a situation where there is a very strong possibility that he may not make it to the other side. He has to decide instantly whether the given task and objective is worth the risk of losing life or limb and go forward unflinchingly, conquering his fear with the overall aim in mind.

If one has been under fire under similar circumstances one can understand perhaps, only slightly, the feelings of those men who fought in the First World War over bullet-and-shell-raked ground between the trench systems, to be mown down in their thousands.

Then there are other manifestations of physical courage, perhaps even more difficult to fathom and of an equally high, if not higher, order of the courage displayed by men under fire.

I think particularly of those men who have become severely handicapped, because of wounds, or even of those born handicapped or being made so because of sickness.

A man who can pick up the pieces when he has been blinded and has lost most of the use of his two hands, as happened to Jack long after Savannah came to an end, is indeed courageous. Jack is still a very useful member of the army, doing what he loves to do, being a soldier – even if by force of circumstances he is forced to drive a desk in his old unit. But he is cheerful all the same.

I shall never forget the day he was taken up in hospital with his very severe injuries. He was in intensive care for a while and I was, quite honestly, reluctant to visit this wreck of a man, wanting to remember him as he was during Savannah, a dashing and brave company commander. I was thinking of myself and not of Jack.

In the end I went because it was my duty and I came back refreshed. Jack was lying on his back, his face, eyes and the stumps of his hands bandaged, and he was talking about the future, what he proposed to do when getting back to his unit, and asking me numerous questions about myself and my family's welfare, offering no comment on his own situation.

He did all the talking and in the end we joked rather irreverently about his injuries.

Later in my military career one of my corporals was blown up by a mine. After weeks of agony, first one and then the other leg was amputated, the first just above and the second just below the knee. He was a paratrooper and his greatest love is skydiving. He decided that come what may, he would skydive again. As soon as he could get up he started to walk on his artificial legs, refusing to use crutches. When discharged from hospital, he did his first free-fall parachute jump, without his legs, during his sick leave. When he came back from sick leave, he stowed away in an aircraft taking paratroopers to the border area for operations against SWAPO. Of course he was aided and abetted by his paratrooper pals.

It was with amazement that we heard that this fellow was seen deep in Angola (in a mechanised column, it must be admitted), moving around on his artificial legs.

Men like that deserve to be decorated, but in our system and in the system of most armies, there is no reward for this kind of courage.

Some men display bravery under fire day after day, for days on end, and then suddenly they crack. We all probably have a certain reserve of courage on which we can draw, but if it is not replenished through rest or training away from the firing line, we may run out of this very useful commodity. A company, hard and proven in battle, may refuse to launch yet another attack or, even worse, go about it in a certain lackadaisical or devil-may-care manner, virtually like zombies.

Some people call this battle fatigue, meaning that all one's senses, including that of the awareness of danger, may become dulled under the constant terrifying hammer blows one is receiving.

Obviously some men can keep going much longer than others and never seem to break. I believe, however, that every man has his capacity for punishment. A leader must watch out for signs of battle fatigue in order to take the necessary action before a soldier, or a body of soldiers, reach breaking point beyond which it is almost impossible to repair the damage done.

My paratrooper on the B-10 at Catengue fought bravely from nine in the morning till six in the evening, being under constant fire. When an additional task was given to him, to be executed away from the main body and during the hours of darkness, the fear that he suppressed all day overcame his resistance and he broke.

The next day, filled with remorse and shame, he plucked up his courage – this time moral courage – to face my inevitable scorn and wrath and very probably disciplinary action for cowardice in the face of the enemy, and admitted honestly and without beating about the bush that he refused to take up his post because he was scared. He could have given all sorts of excuses and it would have been difficult to prove otherwise. He could have feigned illness, or said that he got lost in the dark, or that he must have misheard me.

But he did not. He looked at himself and decided that he was scared and he was willing to admit it. This is an excellent example of moral courage.

There are other examples too, especially in an organisation like an army where the command system is based on an autocracy.

It takes a man of mettle to stand up to a senior and to state one's opinion or case, which may be in direct opposition to that of the superior. Some superior officers also make it harder for the junior by a certain intolerance to the viewpoints of others.

Unfortunately, men of moral courage are rather scarce in conference rooms. Many times I have seen officers trying to anticipate the views of the general. They become part masters at reading his mind and through judicious remarks determining which way the wind is blowing. When the general airs his views, they are in full agreement, some even going so far as to unobtrusively pay compliments to the general's sharpness of mind.

Under those conditions it takes a special kind of courage to stand up and point out, particularly if one is very junior, that the decision reached or about to be reached, is wrong. All those beaming eyes, previously beaming at the general, become as cold as stone as they stare at the upstart in silence. Soon those who supported the general most ardently will wade in, boots and all, to cut the presumptuous fellow down to size.

Needless to say, I avoid conferences like the plague, probably because I do not relish that kind of fighting. My reserve of moral courage is rather limited.

Physical courage comes in various shapes and so does moral courage. I am not a psychologist, but have seen courageous men in action, on the battlefield and in the conference room. It still confuses me, however. I cannot see how one can accurately define courage, taking into account all the factors. It is, for instance, quite feasible that the courageous man of today may be the coward of tomorrow.

Sustaining real courage, both moral and physical, is only possible with Divine Assistance. One reads of life in prison behind the Iron Curtain and the outrageous abuse inflicted on people. One factor shines through above all others: those who put their trust in the Almighty God turn their desperate situation into one of triumph, a shining example for others to behold. I believe it is this Divine Assistance that conquers fear and aids men on the battlefield, even though they may be unaware, at the time, of the source of that strength.

TWELVE
Cubale

The day after Catengue the Brigadier arrived by Aztec at the local airstrip. He was chirpy as always and encouraged us to speed up the advance.

We also received a replenishment of ammunition flown in by Dakota, Bravo and Charlie companies as we were completely out of ammunition after the previous day's heavy fighting.

Corky decided that I should move towards Delville in the direction of Benguela, while Delville would move towards us, both clearing up any pockets of resistance along the way.

Delville and I were separated by about 30 kilometres. The tarred road ran through the most delightful ambushing terrain, being confined mostly between two lines of heavily vegetated hills, quite close to the road on both sides.

It was therefore with some trepidation that the leading armoured car troop and infantry platoon led off the advance through these dangerous defiles. In fact, they moved very slowly, not more than about 5 km/h, with the result that I got a bit impatient after the first hour or so.

I suppose rather recklessly, although I was convinced that there were no substantial bodies of "Injuns in them thar hills," I decided to lead the advance in my open Land Cruiser, the vehicle having been repaired the previous night by the armoured car workshop troop.

Unbeknown to me, Delville had decided to do the same from his end so that the two battle groups approached each other at quite a clip.

Suddenly, in a very narrow ravine, I found myself confronted by a camouflaged Land Rover moving at speed around a bend. For a moment I thought FAPLA had decided to have another go at us, but then I recognised Delville, rigged out in his own particular concept of what a commander should wear when he goes to war. He was tanned a deep brown and wore a brown T-shirt with the sleeves torn off, a camouflaged fatigue cap on his head with the peak removed and displaying a large FINA petrol badge on the front, a string of beads around his neck and a pair of camouflaged trousers. He also wore a pair of boots he had probably been issued with as a recruit some 25 years before.

We were extremely happy to see each other and we filled each other in on our respective fights the previous day. Delville was, understandably, chuffed with his very successful ambush and I was perhaps a little bit envious because I have rarely had the opportunity in my military career to spring a good ambush. We turned round and led the way back to Catengue. On the way, Corky told me by radio that my battle group was to move towards Cubale immediately and to take it before nightfall.

I was not too happy as I considered it to be physically impossible to move about 90 kilometres and to attack and secure a big town between three in the afternoon and last light. So when I got to Catengue I advised Corky accordingly and asked him to postpone the operation until the next morning, which he did in the end. It also gave Bravo and Charlie companies a day of rest after the previous day's heavy fighting.

I now had the opportunity to visit Connie and Alpha Company ten kilometres to the east of Catengue.

When I got there I found the company in the most unusual blocking or ambushing position I had ever seen. Connie's troops were spread out on the uphill side of a long straight stretch of road which descended towards a lone granite "koppie". The road disappeared around the foot of the koppie to cross a long and wide plain below Connie's position. The troops, however, were not dug in or even camouflaged, but walked around quite openly, chewing the fat unconcernedly with their buddies.

Next to the road in good firing positions covering the road were two armoured cars and a B-10, the latter manned by paratroopers. Connie proudly informed me that this was his killing group.

On the left of the road, above a very steep drop to the bottom of a kloof, were four or five completely naked blacks who were digging holes at the end of a long line of 30 or so very fresh graves. It must have been the most unusual graveyard in Angola.

On the koppie, at the bottom of the slope, Connie had a small patrol which could see the approaches to his position along the plain beyond. They would inform Connie of any approaching enemy vehicles, and how many Connie could expect, by visual signalling.

FAPLA still did not realise that we were sitting astride their communication lines to Benguela. The movement of vehicles, mostly singly, was therefore quite frequent.

If the approaching vehicle was identified as FAPLA, the armoured car crew and B-10 crew would quickly take up their positions and open fire with one of the weapons, the other acting as backup, as the vehicle laboured up the slope. The rest of the company or the men nearest the shot-up vehicle, now under cover from view, would jump up, remove the bodies or capture those who were not killed and shove the vehicle over the side. The bodies would be delivered to the burial party, who incidentally were captured FAPLA troops, and prisoners would be passed back to Catengue.

Civilians would be apprehended and evacuated to Catengue as well where they became quite a nuisance, angrily insisting that they wanted to continue their journey to Benguela. This of course could not be allowed until the moment arrived for the ambush to be lifted.

Realising that Connie was doing an excellent job, I returned to Catengue to receive final orders from Corky for the next day's attack against Cubale.

I decided to take Alpha and Charlie companies leaving Jack at Catengue to lick his wounds and to act as a reserve should we require one. The next morning we moved out on the road towards Cubale, picking up Connie and his Alpha Company from their ambush position. By this time Connie could proudly point to well over 40 graves by the wayside.

The first town, on the way to Cubale, was a place by the

name of Chaimbambo. According to Dries there was a resident garrison of about 40 FAPLA on the eastern side of the town in some sort of a "quartel".

I decided therefore to let Charlie Company supply one platoon and I added one troop of armoured cars to charge through the town to overpower the garrison with a sudden and violent assault.

I did not want to waste time as Cubale was far, and according to Dries, quite strongly held by FAPLA.

About ten kilometres west of Chaimbambo, we came face to face with a ten-ton Mercedes truck loaded with harvested coffee beans. It was escorted by two policemen. The one turned out to be the Chief of Police in Chaimbambo, a very friendly individual who had given up long ago trying to determine who his bosses were. I was wondering whether anyone was bothering to pay him even though he remained at his post long after the Portuguese had left.

He confirmed the information about the garrison at Chaimbambo and we sent him on his way to Benguela where he no doubt would get his cut for escorting a lorry load of coffee through a very unsettled part of Africa.

At last Chaimbambo was ahead of us. As the road descended into the valley, we could see all the buildings clustered under a fairly high bush-clad hill on the north side of the road. Beyond, the road levelled out onto a fertile plain planted with lucerne.

I stopped the main body of the column with its head just level with the houses of the smallish town on our left and moved on the troop of armoured cars and the platoon of infantry to go and do their bit on the other side of the village.

Chaimbambo reminded me very much of Hanover in the Cape, with the nearest houses strongly resembling Karoo-type houses, about 100 metres from the main road. Most houses had stoeps facing south towards the road. During a second look I noticed that the stoeps were crammed with FAPLA, all waving frantically at us.

Two men detached themselves from the waving troops and came running towards Toon in his armoured car just ahead of me.

"Kamerad Commandante, Kamerad Commandante!" they shouted while grinning from ear to ear and trying to mount Toon's armoured car.

The red-headed monster – there was no one more unlike a Cuban in the whole column than Toon – kept his presence of mind, or maybe he wanted to play me a trick, and he referred them to me without any hesitation.

"I am not the bloody Commandant. There he is in the Land Cruiser!" he said in English and pointed to me.

The two rushed over happily and the leading one grabbed me by the shoulders and gave me a slobbering kiss on both cheeks.

By this time I had recovered my surprise and I grabbed my rifle next to me, pushed the muzzle deep into the FAPLA's midriff and pulled the trigger.

There was an empty click, nothing more. I had a misfire.

Somewhat flustered I asked the FAPLA to let me have his AK-47, which he meekly handed over. This time I did not have the heart to shoot him and merely took both prisoner.

Never before had I seen two men's faces literally drop the whole range from exultation through an expression of confusion and eventually sheer fright in so short a time. They squatted on their haunches next to my vehicle not saying a word but looking very grey in the face.

Meanwhile the mob were still happily waving at us and I now had a hell of a job to get Toon to understand that I wanted his leading cars to open fire.

I pointed frantically at the crowded stoeps and shouted to Toon: "Open fire! They are FAPLAs."

Toon cupped his ear above the noise of his running engine and shouted back, "What did you say?"

"Shoot those bloody FAPLAs!"

"Huh?"

"Dammit Toon! Look at the stoeps! Shoot those FAPLAs!"

"I can't hear you!"

In the end I took my captured FAPLA's AK-47 and opened fire, all by myself, at the waving crowd.

Toon suddenly clicked, disappeared in his turret and soon

the armoured car turrets traversed towards a rapidly vanishing enemy.

We plastered the place with machine-gun fire, also using Oupa's three-inch mortars. I then sent Connie's company through to clear the place while slowly following behind in my Land Cruiser, Toon's armoured car tagging on just behind my right shoulder.

Meanwhile on the other side of town a fierce little battle erupted during which virtually all of the resident garrison were killed by the advance patrol.

The FAPLAs in town, however, were heading for the hills to the north with Connie's men in hot pursuit. Soon Oupa had to cease fire as the troops were getting beyond support range.

Meanwhile our captured FAPLA had turned out to be the FAPLA commander of this particular force. They were on their way to Benguela and they had got to Chaimbambo only minutes before our arrival.

The policeman, who confirmed the resident FAPLA garrison, therefore was completely unaware of the new arrivals when he met us. Lucky for him, or he would have had some explaining to do.

The FAPLA commander now proceeded to give us some target indication and where the most likely spots were that his running troops would head for. In the end he became quite enthusiastic, especially when the mortars and armoured cars were on target.

Such was his loyalty to his subordinate troops and such was the standard of leadership in the FAPLA army. His companion, to his credit, was taking a very dim view of the proceedings and of his erstwhile commander. One could see that by the sour expression on his face.

As the fight progressed through the town from south to north, Toon and I slowly moved forward.

Suddenly a young Portuguese girl came running from a public building, the Post Office in fact, straight for my car. She was the best thing we had seen for months.

In Portuguese she requested permission to go to her home near the railway station. Her father was the station master of the railway station and she had been inside the Post Office when shooting broke out. Since the fight had now moved on she would like to get home as quickly as possible.

I readily gave permission. The result was that the girl got herself firmly and happily ensconced on the front of Toon's armoured car as he gallantly decided that she needed at least an escort to ensure her safety.

Connie got some of his vehicles stuck in the dry bed of the river running through the centre of the town.

I was getting worried that some of the FAPLA would make for Cubale and give them early warning of our approach. As the minutes ticked by, without any sign of Connie's company appearing from the town, I was getting more and more agitated.

The firing had long since ceased and I was raring to go in order to surprise the Cubale garrison. Finally I made my way to the river where I found him quite unconcernedly examining some captured equipment while his men made quite ineffective and desultory attempts to get the lorries out of the sand.

I blew my top and Connie jumped to it to get his company going.

We beetled along at a great speed, stopped for a short while to clear a railway siding at what turned out to be a minor outpost and reached a position some four or five kilometres south of Cubale from where one could get a fair view of the target.

Our FAPLA prisoner informed us that the garrison was probably about 50 strong and that the FAPLA headquarters was situated in a distinctive building at the southern entrance to the town. The bridge just to the south was unprotected.

I carefully looked through borrowed binoculars at Cubale from a slight knoll next to the road and for the first time in the whole campaign decided to go through all the battle drills as prescribed in textbooks in the Infantry School and Army College.

I had already given a warning order. It would be a two-company attack and the necessary steps were being taken to group the armoured cars and infantry.

Just behind the knoll sat my company commanders, Toon, his troop leaders and the mortar and machine-gun platoon leaders, in accordance with prescribed deployment drills, waiting for me to arrive at a plan and to brief them.

Fully aware of the importance of the occasion, I at last got them onto the knoll behind cover, from where they could see the target just beyond the river. I gave them their orders.

Alpha Company would attack the left-hand side of the long narrow town from south to north with the main street through the centre of town as their right boundary. I think the road was inclusive. The outskirts on the western side would be the left boundary.

Grobbie with his Charlie Company would tackle the rest of the town east of the main street, including the railway station. Each company would have two troops of armoured cars.

The start line would be the southern edge of town. To get there both companies would have to rush across the bridge, Alpha leading. They would then turn left off the main tar road to Nova Lisboa along a street skirting the southern edge of town. A section of infantry and one armoured car were to be dropped off at the entrance to each street to be cleared. They had to wait for my command to proceed with clearing operations.

On the way through to his part of the target Connie would shoot up FAPLA headquarters with his leading troop of armoured cars. The house was situated on its own, but commanding the entrance to the main street.

Fingers, with his machine guns, would charge along the road to Nova Lisboa and deploy his machine guns as a cut-off force to the north-east, raking the northern exits from town when required.

Oupa would deploy his mortars just across the bridge, next to the road to provide support fire on call.

I thought it was an excellent plan, arrived at after going through all the required drills. I accordingly gave myself a pat on the back. There were no questions and everybody went off to give their own orders. We were due to kick off in 30 minutes.

The column was out of sight from Cubale. No movement or life could be seen anywhere in the surrounding farming area, which seemed to be covered as far as the eye could see with acres and acres of sisal.

It was about 1500 hours, quite hot, and we were all preparing a quick brew to swallow down the apprehension rising from our guts.

Paul, as usual, could not find firewood and I literally had to lead him to pick it up. He was quite useless in the victualling department.

Finally we moved off, having re-arranged our order of march, hoping to cover the four or five kilometres to Cubale at great speed before FAPLA could react, particularly to man or even blow the bridge.

We crossed the bridge in great style, swung left and dropped off the assault troops as ordered.

Connie shot up FAPLA headquarters with a tremendous roar, smoke and dust.

All were formed up, ready and keen as mustard to move into their respective streets.

I gave the word and the companies moved forward beautifully, straight from the textbook, with the armoured cars following close behind. We were confronted with a turnout of the local population, cheering and clapping as the assault progressed.

I was disgusted. Not a FAPLA was in sight after all my efforts to do it right this time.

We got to the other end without any troubles whatsoever and paused.

Suddenly a flurry of small-arms firing broke out in the vicinity of the bridge at the mortar base plate positions. In spite of all my efforts I could not raise Oupa, so I decided to drive across. The firing died down, however. By the time I got to the mortars, it was all over.

Oupa was grinning from ear to ear. His men had clobbered about thirty-odd FAPLAs who had crossed the bridge behind us, from south to north, evidently a patrol returning from a mission off to the south-east among the sisal farms.

The troops were grinning too, very happy with the PPSHs which they had been issued with in Sá da Bandeira from captured stores, in lieu of their despised Sten guns.

FAPLA bodies were strewn across the grass. So much for my careful plan. The only people who saw any close-quarter combat were the mortars who were not supposed to indulge in that sort of thing, FAPLA certainly did not play the game.

Now, however, there was the possibility that some pockets of FAPLA might be found along a dirt road running south-east from Cubale through the sisal.

Therefore, I dispatched a troop of armoured cars and an infantry platoon to move for about 15 kilometres along that road to flush out any bodies of FAPLA that may be about.

Unbeknown to me, Oupa and Fingers decided to follow the reconnaissance patrol with a small patrol of their own, having got their blood lust up, I suppose. One of the officers requested permission for them to do so, but I refused it out of hand.

Much persuasive talk from Fingers and Oupa no doubt encouraged this particular officer to ignore my decision. The two left, in two Land Rovers, each armed with two Vickers machine guns, to catch up with the patrol ahead.

It was just getting dusk, with the battle group going into a night laager just south of the town, when a tremendous firefight broke out just across the bridge near some farm buildings.

We could see our armoured cars from the returning patrol plastering an area east of the buildings with their 90 mm guns.

Tracer was streaming towards them and I got the impression that the cars were up against quite a sizeable FAPLA force.

Oupa and Fingers were nowhere in sight and I got quite angry because they were needed.

The platoon with the armoured cars was also rather tardy in moving into the attack and it was going to get quite dark in less than 30 minutes. By that time one would like to have the whole scene wrapped up.

I could not make sense out of the troop commander or the platoon leader, so I decided to investigate the situation myself.

Suddenly flames leapt skyward in the presumed FAPLA positions. I got the infantry deploying in extended line on the edge of a grassy pasture and bullied them forward while the cars were giving covering fire with their machine guns.

Then I saw a rather familiar shape that formed the central point of the conflagration ahead. It looked suspiciously like a Vickers machine gun on the back of a burning Land Rover.

My heart sank into my shoes. Unless FAPLA had acquired Vickers machine guns, we had been making a ghastly mistake.

The cars ceased fire on my orders and I drove ahead, hoping against hope that my suspicions would be proved wrong.

But it was not to be. Out of a small copse staggered a blood-spattered Fingers, his one arm badly shot up. Oupa was face down in a ditch, bleeding badly from wounds in the back.

Two of the gunners were killed, some wounded and quite a few missing. Both Land Rovers and the guns were in flames.

According to Fingers they had tried to catch up with the patrol, but they probably took the wrong turning to the east instead of the south-east at a fork in the dirt road. They drove for miles but found nothing and then decided to turn back.

At the same time the patrol had also turned and were on their way back to the area of the fork just south of the farm buildings.

The two groups approached each other, a chance in a million, and reached the area of the fork almost simultaneously. Oupa and Fingers saw the armoured cars in the dusk but identified them as FAPLA and promptly went into action.

The patrol, of course, rapidly deployed and returned fire, heavily and accurately, as Oupa emphatically vouched for, "Hell, sir, the Boers can shoot! I never, ever, want to be at the receiving end of Boer fire again!"

So our Cubale adventure ended on a very sad and somewhat sour note.

I lost two of my best soldiers, Oupa and Fingers, because both had to be evacuated the next day. The mortar and machine-gun platoons were never the same again, the troops in those platoons themselves being thoroughly disheartened at losing two men for whom they had the greatest love and respect.

In due course two new support platoon leaders arrived, but they were not nearly as competent as Oupa and Fingers, nor could they find a rapport with the troops. In the end, I disbanded the two support platoons and absorbed the men in the rifle companies.

THIRTEEN
Benguela

We returned to Catengue early the next morning. Jack and his company had just returned from Chaimbambo where they had cleared the area after our previous day's unforeseen scrap with FAPLA, when we pulled into that town. Apart from Jack and his men, the place was completely deserted.

Delville and his battle group, Zulu headquarters and the whole logistical system had moved on to Benguela. We were to follow on behind, according to Jack.

Jack also gave me some rather bad news. Nic had been killed the previous day in an aircraft accident. I also knew two of the others who were killed: Piet the pilot and Des, an old colleague from Oudtshoorn.

Nic's death, however, touched me very deeply as he was my second in command of the previous unit I had commanded. He was, in fact, more of a friend than a colleague. He also had a tremendous sense of humour, so much so that Nic was known far and wide throughout the Army and Air Force for his sense of fun. He was one officer who would be sorely missed. Even to this day many anecdotes concerning Nic are retold wherever officers, and especially paratroopers, gather over a few beers.

In a way I was glad that Delville and not us would be doing the day's share of fighting. I preferred to mope about Nic in my Land Cruiser, as we were making our way to Benguela.

The hot miles disappeared behind us as the column snaked along through the valleys and defiles towards the coast. Toon pulled level with me in his Land Rover and he passed me a beer, which I drank with gratitude as we drove along, two abreast, while reminiscing about the past.

Soon our spirits perked up and we began to take an interest in the scenery around us.

We passed the scene of Delville's very successful ambush. Burnt-out wrecks from trucks and cars were scattered around all over the place. There was no sign of Zulu Force ahead of us, but we were not concerned.

It was good to relax for awhile without wondering and worrying about the hills ahead and the flanks hiding an unpleasant surprise in the form of a FAPLA ambush.

We passed through the final line of hills, through a narrow defile, where we found an extensive but unoccupied trench system, before emerging onto the coastal plain just south of Benguela.

Ahead we could hear the distant thump of guns and probably rockets. It was obvious that Delville had run into quite a fair-sized fight, judging from the sound.

Toon and I had now stopped reminiscing and we were beginning to feel just a little bit apprehensive when ahead, at the end of a long straight stretch of tar road, we could make out the short round figure of a little man standing in the middle of the road next to his grey short wheel-base Land Rover.

We had caught up with Zulu headquarters and Corky was obviously waiting for us to appear on the scene.

As we drew up, Corky stopped my whole column by simply making like a traffic cop. He looked worried.

Delville, evidently, had picked up trouble on the airport, just south of Benguela. We could hear the almost continuous banging away of heavy guns fairly clearly and could even see the odd column of smoke on the far side of the plain just ahead of us.

Meanwhile FAPLA was reported to be abducting Portuguese families onto deep-sea trawlers from a place called Baía Farta, just down the coast from Benguela.

Corky wanted me to make for Baía Farta to rescue the hostages. The rest of my battle group was to concentrate at the old FAPLA quartel a few miles further on. Delville had kicked FAPLA out of the place earlier in the day.

I detailed a troop of armoured cars and an infantry platoon to come with Toon and myself to Baía Farta. Frank had to take the rest to the concentration area.

So we turned left, off the main Benguela road, and sped along a plain, dotted with barren flat-topped hills, towards the distant sea to the south-west.

The plain reminded me very much of the Karoo – the same barrenness with small Karoo-type scrub, dongas and flat-topped hills. It was also very hot.

Not far from Baía Farta, which we could see in the distance, we came face to face with a Mercedes Benz going towards Benguela. The driver turned out to be a local white Portuguese from the town.

We were glad to hear that there was no truth in the abduction rumours. FAPLA, however, had a small garrison in a single building in the centre of town. He was prepared to act as guide to show us the place.

So the advance continued, this time with the Mercedes Benz just behind my Land Cruiser. We entered Baía Farta, a surprisingly big town which we had never heard of, from the northeast.

The main street was flanked by two-storey buildings and shops, but everything was deserted. Not a soul in the streets. Off to the right was the dockyard area where we could see the tops of masts and rigging of numerous vessels in port.

First we had to clear out FAPLA before we could take a closer look at the place. So, under the expert guidance of our Portuguese friend, we finally arrived at the FAPLA quartel.

It was of rather disappointing appearance. In fact it was the most unprepossessing "quartel" I had yet seen in the war so far. It was nothing but an ordinary four- or five-bedroomed house. No barbed wire, no machine-gun nests, no imposing-looking fortifications built of sandbags or concrete.

Unbelieving, I questioned my Portuguese informer again. There was no doubt about it. This was the quartel and the FAPLAs were definitely inside according to him. They were probably looking at us through the windows and could start shooting at any moment.

With disbelief I looked at the peaceful scene in front of me but decided that discretion would be the better part of valour. We would do a proper little clearing operation on the premises.

The trouble was that although we had fought through quite a few towns, we never really had to do house clearing. We did some in Pereira de Eça, but that was very much a hit-and-miss affair. I had also not had the time, or opportunity, to give my troops proper training in house clearing.

So here was the golden opportunity, presented to me on a plate. I would use the FAPLA house to teach the infantry platoon house clearing and I would act as instructor and also demonstrate how it was to be done.

A 90 mm armoured car was parked on each corner of the house. No FAPLA was going to take the gap as far as I was concerned.

The infantry platoon was dismounted and I briefly explained to them what I was about to do. They nodded and smiled. This was going to be fun! With myself, the platoon leader and one or two other troops, we entered the front door of the house, which opened onto a passage. Unexpectedly, the Portuguese civilian had decided to accompany us, but it was too late to chase him back.

We were committed as the house-clearing party. The door to the first room on the right was shut. We had no hand grenades, none in fact in the whole of Bravo Group, so that we were forced to rely on our rifles only.

Now I had been in the army for many years, trained hard to become a reasonably proficient infantry man, even to clear houses, but I had also seen a few war films with John Wayne and others, who to my mind gave a far better demonstration of how a house should be cleared than the army ever did.

So I kicked the door open and stormed in, my rifle at my hip, ready to blast FAPLA to smithereens. The room was empty. Disappointed I moved up the passage to the next room on the left. Somewhere in the innards of the house I was bound to come across FAPLA and my dander was well and truly up. The next door was also shut. It was, in fact, well and truly locked, or so I thought. So I took a mighty kick at it and nearly broke my leg. It made no impression.

Meanwhile the Portuguese was mumbling something about "Kameraden" while pointing at the door. It was obvious to me therefore that FAPLA would be hiding in that room. All I had to do was get the door open, charge in and empty my magazine into the terrified FAPLA troops. John Wayne showed the way, so I stood back and charged the door with my shoulder with great determination.

I bounced off the door like a rag doll and fell flat on my backside. The demonstration was getting just a little bit out of hand and I was beginning to lose my cool, having noticed surreptitious smirks on the faces of the rest of the party .

The Portuguese was going frantic. "Kameraden!" he shouted, pointing at the door.

"Yes, I know, dammit. I'll get them out one way or another!" I shouted back at him. I tried another John Wayne trick. I emptied my magazine through the door and tried to shoot off the lock. The Portuguese was having a fit "Kameraden! Kameraden! Not schiessen!" The latter in broken English and German.

I was just about to have another go at the door when I saw the catch turning very slowly. That was indeed strange. The door opened a crack and a black frightened face peered through the crack at me. Suddenly the face smiled and the door was thrown wide open. It was one of my own troops!

Some of them had decided to ignore my demonstration and they had decided to start their own version of house clearing from the other side. I felt a damn fool, needless to say, but tried to keep my pose, which was somewhat difficult in front of my own little house-clearing party. They had actually seen John Wayne in action.

The house was empty, so we went off to the docks to check up on the hostage rumours. We went on board several deep-sea trawlers, very well appointed ships they were too, and found that the crews had prudently moved their families on board, for a quick getaway if necessary.

The Portuguese guide gave us a bag of coal as a parting gesture. Maybe the gift expressed what he thought of my house-clearing demonstration or, maybe, coal was so scarce in Baía Farta that it was in fact a very valuable present; I wouldn't know, but I accepted it with thanks and left Baía Farta as quickly as possible.

We rolled into the concentration area as the sun was going down. Frank had deployed Bravo Group in a defensive circle, more or less manning the embankments of the old quartel. Zulu headquarters was pulled up under the northern embankment.

Off to the north, Red Eye rockets were mushrooming between us and Delville on the airport. A lot of machine gun and rifle fire came from that direction. Delville was obviously having a rough time and night was coming on fast.

I found a spot inside the quartel, less dirty than most other spots, where I parked the Land Cruiser and proceeded to Zulu headquarters.

The quartel had earlier been occupied by Cubans. Some equipment, rifles, ammunition and a lot of mines had been captured by Delville inside the quartel. The place was, however, one big filthy mess. The Cubans had no idea whatsoever of hygiene. They in fact "crapped" inside and outside the quartel, on top of the embankments, inside the few buildings and, it seemed to me, wherever the urge took them. The place stank!

Corky could not use any of the buildings as headquarters because of the filth and the fleas. He therefore pitched his headquarters away from the buildings in an open spot.

There was no doubt that Benguela would be a very tough nut to crack, mainly because it is a largish city with numerous multi-storeyed buildings and large shanty towns tacked onto the side of it.

Delville had not been able to clear the airport because he was brought under rocket fire from high ground north of Benguela and under small-arms and mortar fire from the city itself. His troops were all pinned down at the airport and behind the air terminal buildings.

Corky visited the airfield during the day to be able to plan our actions. He refused to be pinned down at the airfield forever and we discussed various possible attacks. An outflanking attack round the east would be in full view of the observation post officers of the mortars and the rockets that have harassed us all day. A direct attack on the city was not feasible as the city was too big, there were too many civilians and it would most certainly develop into the most horrible and costly form of warfare, namely street fighting. Corky eventually suggested a limited attack on the outskirts of the town bordering the airfield to quell the direct fire being brought down on us. That would make us retain the initiative and allow us time to plan subsequent actions.

Eventually we decided that it would be better to try and outflank Benguela to the east and attack the high ground north of the city. That would cut off FAPLA's retreat and put us on dominating terrain. It would also neutralise the FAPLA rocket batteries.

It was agreed that I would send a patrol to find a route around the east and a ford through the river that ran into the sea just south of the high ground. The river was in flood as the rainy season had started inland.

After evening conference, Corky opened a bottle of Smirnoff, one of the few we received from Rundu, and which he evidently saved for a suitable occasion. Delville complained about his Portuguese platoon leaders, but nobody took any notice. The Smirnoff gradually made our surroundings – and the smell – more acceptable and I soon turned in despite the odd Red Eye going off from time to time.

My patrol went off early the next morning to find a passage around the east flank, to no avail, however, as there was no suitable river crossing.

The firing had picked up again towards daybreak and Delville had left just as rocket fire was beginning to mushroom between us and the airport.

The Smirnoff had worn off and I was looking in the cold light of morning at the general situation in the enemy training camp where I had slept the previous night. I was disgusted. Bits of human excrement could be found everywhere and I felt as if I was covered in fleas.

I therefore decided to take my chance with Delville and departed for the airport, waving gravely at Corky as I passed his headquarters.

Keeping the air terminal building between me and FAPLA in the city made it possible to drive right up to Delville's headquarters. He was on the top floor, in fact an open balcony, from where he had a bird's-eye view of the city and could also see the rocket positions on the high ground to the north.

The trouble was that he had nothing with which he could reach the Stalin Organs, not even with the 81 mm mortars.

All around us his Bushmen were lying behind cover, hammering away across a stretch of open ground at the nearest buildings of the city.

Groups of armoured cars were clustered up and down the airfield from where they added to the din with their 90 mm guns.

Suddenly an unmarked Dakota appeared over the city, heading for the airport. For a while everybody stopped shooting and then all opened up on the Dakota, FAPLA and the Bushmen.

We were a bit puzzled by its identity, but Delville got his troops to stop shooting as the aircraft was obviously going to land. If it was a FAPLA aircraft, we could capture it on the ground.

The Dakota landed and unconcernedly taxied to the dispersal area behind the terminal building. It was one of our own Dakotas.

Firing had picked up again between the Bushmen and FAPLA so that bullets, interspersed with rockets and mortars, were flying around all over the airfield.

The pilot sat for a while, waiting for somebody to offload his machine but, as nothing happened (fighting kept everybody busy), he decided that he and his crew had better do it, and quickly too. Soon ammunition boxes tumbled out of the rear. By this time the pilot must have realised that we were still fighting for the airport and that he had landed right in the middle of a firefight. Never had an aircraft been cleared so quickly. Within minutes the engines started up again, the Dakota turned around and commenced its take-off run from dispersal across the rough veld, ignoring all runways or taxiways. It soon disappeared over the horizon towards the south.

Meanwhile Delville and I were having a second look at the air photographs of Benguela. It was obvious that the high ground north of the town had to be taken. Outflanking to the east of Benguela was out of the question as we could not cross the flooded river. The only way across was by means of the bridge just north of the main city centre.

In order to take the high ground, we would have to clear at least part of Benguela, that part just north of the airfield, so that the 81 mm mortars could be deployed within range of our final objective, the rocket batteries.

We had arrived, at least partially, at Corky's solution. Corky was, understandably, disgusted that we, Delville and I, had decided to adopt his plan after our strenuous objections the previous night.

While all this planning was going on, FAPLA was trying very hard indeed to wipe Delville's headquarters off the face of the earth with some rocket fire. Delville therefore placed one of his men as a lookout for incoming rockets while he and I studied the air photographs.

Every now and again a warning would sound "Here it comes!" followed by Delville's comment "Here comes a pot of crap".

We would take cover, wait for the explosions and carry on with our planning. Finally FAPLA decided to let go a whole broadside of rockets from the other side. "Here it comes, a whole lot of them!" followed by Delville's comment: "Here comes a big pot of crap!"

We took cover. Rockets exploded all around the headquarters, the building shook, dust and smoke covered us and when it finally blew away we were still in one piece. The spent rocket motors could be seen sticking out of the ground just in front and behind the terminal building, looking for all the world like the army's well-known urinal "lillies".

We decided that I would clear the shanty town to the immediate north with two of my companies while Delville would give fire support. Afterwards Delville's Bushmen would leapfrog through and clear the rest of the town while the mortars would redeploy. The final assault would be done by Delville – to take the high ground to the north.

Frank brought up two of my companies and the remainder of Toon's armoured cars. I joined the companies and we assaulted from east to west across Delville's front, Jack's company on the left and Connie's company on the right.

Corky had joined Delville at his command post from where they had a beautiful view of my companies moving through the outskirts of Benguela.

It looked good; my troops moved well with the armoured cars a short step behind to give immediate and close support where necessary. Unfortunately, there was no resistance, FAPLA had gapped it as soon as we started deploying.

So we decided to clear all Benguela.

Jack's company was detailed to clear the southern approaches and the centre of town, afterwards to cross the river and to make for the high ground in the north.

Connie's company was to clear the eastern side of Benguela as far as the river.

Gradually the streets began to fill with people and by the time Jack got to the centre of the city, the streets were thronged with wildly cheering inhabitants. He could not carry on with his clearing actions as he was virtually bogged down in the crowds.

Jack therefore requested permission to open fire over the heads of the crowds to disperse them so that he could get his company moving again.

I was flabbergasted and quickly stopped Jack. I instructed him to ignore the city centre, to drive through in a victorious procession, to accept the flowers, the beer and the cheers and to make for the high ground to the north.

Meanwhile I made my way to the centre of the city. Everything was in uproar. People stretched out their hands to touch the liberators. Others ran next to the vehicles and spouted away in Portuguese. The troops beamed from ear to ear, especially at the girls.

Connie had cleared his area with far more decorum than Jack, and I instructed him to pull into a very beautifully situated cemetery on high ground, surrounded by thick stone walls, for the night. It was a very strong position, but the troops were somewhat apprehensive about spending a night among the dead of Benguela.

Jack got to the high ground north of the city. The bird had flown and left some entrenchments, rockets, empty boxes and so on behind. They were obviously heading for Lobito.

I slept behind Delville's command post that night. There was no way in which anybody was going to get me back into the Cuban quartel for my last night in Benguela; even if odd bodies of FAPLA could still be running around the airport or in the city, intent on having a go at the widely separated bodies of Zulu troops, cut off from each other by dark and intervening blocks of buildings over which we had no control for the moment.

FOURTEEN
Marking Time

We were supposed to leave the next morning by eight, but we had discovered an abandoned restaurant, just south of the driveway to the airport, stocked with all sorts of goodies we had not seen for ages. There were huge whole crayfish in the deep freeze, beautiful fillet steaks, sausages, all sorts of makings for salads and last, but definitely not least, bottles of white and red wine.

Unfortunately, we only came across this just before our scheduled time of departure for Lobito. It did not worry me too much though, as Delville was leading the advance.

So Bravo Group got stuck into the most fantastic breakfast: crayfish followed by perfectly done fillet steaks, all washed down with bottles of white and red wine and finally followed by cups of strong coffee.

Thousands of packets of cigars, evidently issued to Cuban troops, had been captured, so, replete with all the good fare, those who smoked lit up their fat cigars and leisurely made their way to their vehicles.

It was about nine o'clock when I finally got the show on the road. I went ahead to have a look at the high ground beyond the city, as well as FAPLA's rocket positions the previous day.

There were some abandoned 122 mm rockets and lots of empty boxes, but no sign of any abandoned weaponry.

Just beyond the crest of the high ground was a little church with a priest still *in situ* – the first priest we had seen till then – and some quite respectable-looking houses.

I waited for Bravo to catch up, and with Toon as my passenger we led the whole procession through mile after mile of sugar cane, obviously irrigated as the rainfall is very low along the coast.

On our left was the blue Atlantic with miles of deserted beaches, a vast potential for tourism.

From time to time we would cross a fiercely flooding river, the rains inland having started. They were flowing in a chocolate-brown flood into the sea.

Next to the road ran the famous Benguela railway, which actually starts in Lobito and not in Benguela.

Rumour had it that FAPLA had taken up positions just beyond one of the flooding rivers, halfway to Lobito, on prominent high ground that dominated all of the approaches from the south. This was Delville's problem, not ours. Toon and I were at peace with the world, having fed really well for the first time since the campaign started.

And so we arrived on the southern outskirts of Lobito. Not a shot was being fired, no angry-looking armoured cars were moving into firing positions. In fact, we had been meeting truckloads of jubilant Lobitans who had come out of the city to meet us.

This, of course, was the signal for my men to display their large FNLA banners from every lorry. Portuguese was shouted backwards and forwards between my troops and the Lobitans. People laughed and sang and come-hither remarks were no doubt made on both sides.

I could smell trouble ahead so decided, there and then, not to stop in Lobito but to drive straight through until I reached a spot at least 30 kilometres beyond, even if I had to fight FAPLA to secure a camping site.

The flesh pots of Lobito would be too much for my troops. I had my doubts whether I would see any of them afterwards.

We entered the city proper, passing the airport on our left. The streets were thronged with wildly cheering crowds. I had problems forging through the masses with my Land Cruiser. Hands were extended to be shaken. People laughed, danced and sang. One chap even ran after us with his girlfriend, which he deposited on my Land Cruiser. "She is yours!" he shouted in English. I made her understand that we were heading for a place far to the north of Lobito and she had better get off or else she would be going to war. Luckily she believed me and jumped off after a block or two.

We passed the completely wrecked MPLA headquarters. Evidently that very morning, without any prompting, the Lobito population had attacked MPLA and driven them out of the city. I was told later that quite a number of MPLA officials were killed.

The multi-storeyed building was a mess of broken glass. Broken furniture littered the street. Here and there fires were smouldering after attempts to burn the place down. Several bodies could be seen lying on the pavement, whether they were locals or MPLA was difficult to say.

At the harbour we turned right and followed the road out of town winding upwards to the top of the escarpment until it finally swung north again, parallel to the sea on our left.

The rejoicing among the troops gradually diminished in volume until there was a deathly hush as Lobito fell behind us, thus also the promised flesh pots.

On the way I passed Delville and his Alpha Group. He obviously had come to the same conclusion as I had. We drove on another 12 kilometres, turned off the main road and made camp for the night on an abandoned farm. There was no sign of FAPLA, only rumours from the local population that FAPLA had passed earlier that morning in a great hurry and that some of them had come to grief in a mountain pass further north where landslides had caused some vehicles to end at the bottom of a ravine.

I sent a patrol of infantry and armoured cars in that direction, but they came back without making any contact or seeing any sign of FAPLA.

The troops were not overjoyed with the fact that Lobito was about 30 kilometres to the south, but they made the best of a bad situation.

I sent Danny back with a platoon to secure the dockyard area and especially the fuel tanks. We were bargaining on capturing the fuel at Lobito to sustain our further advance up the coast.

I went back with Toon to the airport at Lobito, which had become the site for Zulu headquarters, to report to Corky and to receive further instructions. According to Corky we would be marking time until the powers that be had decided whether we should go for Luanda or whether we should be satisfied with what we had and just consolidate our position.

November 11, the official date on which Angola would become independent, was just around the corner. We already had most of Angola in our grip, certainly the most important part of it, including the Benguela railway line. That of course also included FNLA's conquests in the northern provinces adjacent to Zaire.

When I returned to our laagering area, I found a very irate Danny waiting for me. He had returned with his platoon from the fuel tanks in Lobito where he had been thoroughly beaten up. Danny told me that they were hardly in position when a whole bunch of UNITA troops turned up at the dockyard. They had followed us into Lobito and were under the command of a fellow called Lumumba. With a war name like Lumumba it could mean only one thing. This fellow would not be a friend of FNLA and certainly not of any South African. Danny was peremptorily ordered to vacate the dockyard.

He objected, quite rightly claiming that he only took orders from me and that Lumumba had to discuss the matter with me. Lumumba's reply was that he would only talk to me if he wanted to buy a pocket of potatoes, which only served to make Danny lose his temper. He no doubt said some unflattering things about UNITA whereupon UNITA, on the orders of Lumumba, proceeded to beat up Danny and the few men he had with him at the time.

I saw red at this calculated insult of a UNITA commander. By this time after our little differences of opinion at Caungar, Cuvelai and Artur de Paiva, I was more than just a little bit prejudiced against our UNITA allies. My own FNLA troops also cleverly knew when to stoke the fires.

I ordered two armoured cars to come with me. I was going to find Lumumba and I was going to rid Lobito of his continued presence.

So in a boiling mood I made my way back to Lobito, stopping off at Delville's position to inform him of my intentions. He, in his turn, was on his way to go and sort out another UNITA leader called Dr Valentino. Evidently UNITA elements under Valentino's command had assaulted one of his platoons while on their legitimate business, also in the dockyard area.

I made my way to the quartel in an old fort on top of the escarpment overlooking the harbour city of Lobito. There I found a large number of UNITA troops busy looting the place.

Paul had been left behind, so I tried to make myself understood in English. I was also very angry and therefore somewhat reckless as I grabbed a likely looking UNITA troop by the shoulder.

"Where is that clot Lumumba? I want him!"

About 20 or 30 troops were pressing around us and my armoured cars were nowhere in sight. "I don't know boss. He is not here. Maybe he has gone to the radio station," said the wide-eyed troop in Afrikaans.

"You are a SWAPO because only SWAPO can speak Afrikaans!"

"No boss, I am UNITA, not SWAPO!"

There was a lot of ill-tempered mumbling among the troops, so I decided to leave. At the bottom of the hill I found one armoured car in a ditch with the other trying to pull it out. This did not improve my temper because I could have been killed up there with no armoured cars anywhere in sight to give support. I ordered the cars to follow me as soon as they had managed to dig themselves out and I went to the radio station.

The fellow in charge turned out to be a white Portuguese. He also had several white assistants. All were adamant that Dr Valentino was extremely bad news for Lobito.

When Lobito had been under UNITA control some month's before, Valentino had been the governor of the area. His idea of spreading the gospel according to Dr Savimbi was to lock up dissenters and to torture them until they recanted and became UNITA supporters.

It was obvious that Lobito was not a haven of UNITA supporters. On the contrary: they seemed mostly to support FNLA, thus the joyous display of support earlier in the day.

The last the crew of the radio station had seen of Valentino during UNITA's previous occupation was when he was frantically rowing for a ship in the harbour as FAPLA entered the town on the landward side. They were very unhappy to see him back.

Anyway, my quarrel was with Lumumba, not Valentino. They informed me, however, that Lumumba will probably accompany Valentino to the radio station. They were expecting him at about nine p.m. as he wanted to make a statement to the people of Lobito. They were, in fact, standing by for him. So I decided to stand by also but for Lumumba, not for Valentino.

Nine o'clock came and went but there was no sign of either Lumumba or Valentino. By this time the two armoured cars had joined me again. I was not prepared to wait any longer and decided to look for him elsewhere in town.

The radio station crew informed me that Lumumba and Valentino were supposed to have dinner at the only hotel still operating before they were to come to the radio station.

At the hotel they told me that Valentino and Lumumba had dined earlier on but that they had gone to the airport. My procession stormed to the airport, which was then also Zulu headquarters.

Everything was very quiet in the terminal building, but I started to search the place from top to bottom. Eventually I found two UNITA gentlemen in deep conversation with Corky in the baggage area of the building.

By this time I was ready to blow a gasket, having waited for hours around Lobito for Lumumba to turn up. The waiting did not improve my temper. In fact, the radio station crew had added fuel to the fire. So I cocked my rifle and demanded angrily, "Which of you two bastards is Lumumba?" Corky was caught off balance and flabbergasted.

"Why do you want to know?" he demanded.

"Because if I find out which one it is I am going to shoot him."

Valentino spoke perfect English and he was going grey in the face as he began to stutter. "It must be a mistake." He turned out to be the fat one with the glasses.

Slightly behind him stood a perfectly dumb-looking idiot who obviously had no comprehension of what was going on. That had to be Lumumba, so I turned my rifle on him.

"Stop you bloody fool! You are wrecking my whole diplomatic effort!" shouted Corky as he moved in between me and Lumumba.

"Get out! I now have to start all over again."

The little man was understandably very angry.

"But this bastard assaulted my troops at the dockyard!"

"We'll discuss it later. Get out!"

So I left with my tail between my legs. As I left, Delville stormed in there as well, having looked for Valentino all over Lobito and finally running him down at the airport. He was going to kill Valentino, not Lumumba, so that the same performance was being repeated with different actors. Poor old Corky was having a rough time that night with his battle group commanders.

The next morning Delville, Toon, Frank and I went back to headquarters. The high brass was arriving that morning to discuss future operations.

Toon and I went in my Land Cruiser, Frank in his own and Delville in his Land Rover, the whole of Zulu Force upper hierarchy looking somewhat disreputable, most having grown beards. Delville looked particularly outlandish in his strange garb.

Soon from inland a group of armoured cars arrived: Eddie, the boss man of battle group Foxbat, and his staff with Holly, his second in command, in his own armoured car.

The Eighth Army and First Army were meeting after many months of campaigning, the Eighth Army feeling and looking somewhat superior with an air of "devil-may-care" in their assorted looted vehicles and different modes of dress. No doubt the First Army felt superior also when noticing our lack of military bearing and conformity. They looked much smarter in their olive green fatigues and with their beautiful armoured cars.

Eddie, however, gave us a demonstration with his M79 grenade launcher, the first time most of us had seen one. It was a very effective little weapon, throwing 40 mms HE rounds up to a range of 200 metres. Eddie was using it as his personal weapon.

Holly was his usual self, a perfectionist as always and thoroughly enjoying the war.

Foxbat had been pushing northwards from Nova Lisboa and they had cleared the lateral road between Lobito and Alto Hama so that lateral communications between Foxbat and Zulu was now possible.

A C-160 appeared in the circuit and we all adjourned to the airport building to watch the landing. The C-160 was bringing the high brass from the south.

It also brought a load of beer, the first actually flown in to the troops. Up till then we had to rely on the odd case coming in with the Dakota, although I am sure Toon had some sort of secret arrangement. He always seemed to have a supply of Castle beer.

When the ramp opened, Toon and I spotted the cases of beer, like manna from heaven. We promptly forgot all about the brass and made for the C-160.

There must have been at least a hundred cases of beer and we promptly claimed a bottle each and proceeded to drink thirstily while sitting on the ramp of the aircraft.

It was Angolan beer, somewhat fresh, from the distillery in Sá da Bandeira. Boy, a friend of ours, and a sort of military governor for Sá da Bandeira had got his priorities right. One of the first things he did was to get the brewery going again. Bless old Boy!

The brass was not very impressed as they watched Toon and myself putting away our beers. They wanted to get on with the conference.

Finally we made our way to the restaurant area. New faces were John, Coen, Smokey and Toutjies. Coen had come to join Delville as second in command. Smokey had brought a troop of 25-pounder guns. FAPLA was going to have a rough time from now on. The guns had been offloaded at Benguela and were on their way. Toutjies had come to polish off the few bottles of whisky Coen brought through and to look at some gunnery problems, in that order. Johan was the new commander of I Military Area and was on an orientation trip. The Brigadier was the boss we had met before.

So we discussed further operations in a relaxed atmosphere, the Brigadier as pleased as punch with the progress so far.

It had been decided to keep pushing up the coast as far as Porto Amboim to the north, then to turn eastwards for Gabela and Quibala to join up with Foxbat who would be thrusting up the centre towards Quibala. We were evidently on our way to Luanda. Fresh troops were being deployed from South Africa and the whole campaign was beginning to look more South African than Angolan. A new battle group was being formed or was about to be formed, which was to be called X-ray. They would clear the railway line eastwards from Luso, a big railway town in the hands of UNITA. Another force, Yankee, would be moving north, further eastwards from Foxbat to make for the bridge over the Cuanza River at Malanje. Lobito would become a log base where ships from the south could offload whatever was required for the war effort.

The military effort was therefore expanding instead of being diminished as some of us had thought. We would certainly not be leaving Angola on the eleventh. Later in the day Delville, Toon and I borrowed Corky's black Mercedes Benz to go and have dinner in town, in style.

We went to the same hotel where I had looked for Lumumba the previous night. With Delville's direction – he had been to Lobito previously and could speak Portuguese – we had a fairly good dinner, keeping in mind that the war had enforced some austerity on the population.

Lobito used to be the major seaport of Angola. I don't know whether it still is. It is, of course, firmly tied to the Benguela railway line which nowadays does not operate because of the unhealthy fascination the line has for UNITA.

It was also the major holiday resort for at least central and southern Angola, the central part being really the heartland. It contained the largest concentration of well-to-do Portuguese settlers before they were forced to flee back to Portugal.

Lobito therefore had quite a nightlife with nightclubs, strip clubs, carnivals and beauty competitions, apart from the splendid swimming on secluded beaches and sailing and boating in the natural harbour.

The night we went out on the town the only facility that was still in operation, and that only at half cock, was the hotel.

We pretended that it was, for tired warriors, the best entertainment we had for ages. And so we returned to our respective camps in a good mood, having forgotten all about Lumumba and Valentino.

The next day we decided to explore the coast further to the north and we found a small seaside resort. The troops were promptly packed off to this place for a good swim and lazing around on the beach. Beer was provided from the previous day's consignment.

It seemed that the resort was owned by a single Portuguese family, still *in situ* and waiting for better days. Presumably a charge would be made for entrance to the beach, but in this instance the owner waived it, being glad that better days had finally arrived.

So we swam in a majestic setting of tall cliffs with long stretches of empty white beach at our feet. The water was clear and if we had scuba gear we would have enjoyed it more, because there seemed to be interesting reefs offshore. According to the owner the place teemed with fish. There was a small fishing village just visible to the south to prove the point.

We were supposed to move off the next day for Novo Redondo, Delville leading again with us following in the early afternoon.

As we had not seen any of the beachfront of Lobito, Toon and I decided to do a little bit of exploring in his Land Rover. We set off the next morning down the bluff, sheltering the natural harbour on the Atlantic side, to the beaches which Delville claimed was the centre of attraction for all of Lobito.

We followed the main road, flanked by beautiful houses, gardens and parks to the point of the bluff. To our right was the tranquil water of the harbour, a few ships alongside and one or two anchored out in the roadstead. They seemed quite unconcerned about the war.

I noticed the same about engine drivers. A battle would be fought, whether in Sá da Bandeira, Moçâmedes, Benguela, Lobito or elsewhere and the trains would come and go quite unconcernedly, sticking to their timetables. Many was the time that we would pass a train on its way either to or from the direction of the enemy, on a railway line running alongside the road we were moving on, with our very ferocious looking, war-like column of armoured cars and troop carrying vehicles.

We would wave to the driver and the driver would cheerfully wave back. Somehow it never occurred to us to stop the train, probably because it would be an unheard of thing to do in South Africa, in order to find out about conditions further along the railway line. We finally arrived at the point of the bluff where the best beaches were reputed to be.

We sat on the seawall and looked at the scenery. Beautiful palm trees lined the beaches, each enclosed within walls running into the sea, thus forming a whole series of secluded little beaches instead of one long one on which the surf could pound away without restriction. The walls were probably there to prevent the gradual erosion of the narrow bluff.

The small beach ahead of us also contained two young bikini-clad girls splashing around in the shallow water.

The girls spotted the two strange characters sipping beer on the seawall. They left the water and came gliding across the sand towards us.

They came to a halt in front of us. One was a brunette and the other had red hair. The one with red hair enquired about our reasons for being in Angola and wanted to know who we were.

Before Toon could answer I made the introductions. "My name is Gardiner. I come from Rhodesia. My friend here is a Dutchman from Holland by the name of Koekemoer. Unfortunately, he cannot speak English, but I am willing to translate if you want me to."

The red-haired girl glanced at Toon. He would not be able to talk to her much as he wanted to, for fear of compromising our cover story.

The girl and I discussed the war, UNITA – of which she was a member – and other important matters. After a while I decided that Toon must be "brought up to date".

"Excuse me, I want to translate for my friend." I said to her.

"Toon, look at that build and that belly button. Don't you think she is gorgeous?" She was standing more or less in line with me with her belly button at just about eye level.

"You know, you are a real bastard. I will never go anywhere with you again. You know how to spoil a man's day." This was from Toon, in Afrikaans to keep up appearances.

"My friend says he agrees wholeheartedly with your impressions of the war and the political situation, but quite frankly, his concept of what is going on in Angola is somewhat hazy! He fights for money, you see," I said to the girl.

She looked at Toon with disapproval, while Toon was getting redder than his normal beetroot colour. Finally we gave the two girls a can of beer each. They undulated back to their "suntan" position under the palms while he stared after them with some regret.

We got into the Land Rover and returned to the troops to start moving towards further clashes of arms with FAPLA to the north.

We were not sorry to get underway again. My run-in with Lumumba and Corky's consequent ire and the lack of action while FAPLA was getting further away to the north – no doubt preparing their defences against our advance – made me glad to be on the move again.

We certainly were giving them enough time to catch their breath after the pounding they received at Benguela and further south.

Next time we were going to run into well-organised defensive systems. The four days' break, though welcome for resting the troops, could turn out to be a big mistake in the end.

FIFTEEN
Novo Redondo

And so it was to be. Delville's Bushmen had run into a very nasty situation by the time Bravo Group, tail-end Charlie for the moment, pulled out of Lobito.

To the north, about 20 kilometres south of Novo Redondo, a rather large river breaks out of a very narrow gorge into a plain that is about five to eight kilometres wide before emptying its muddy water into the Atlantic.

To the south and north of this plain, the escarpment reaches right up to the sea so that the plain forms a sort of indentation in the line of cliffs. The cliff face has receded inland over thousands of years of constant eroding by the rushing waters of the river.

Delville had entered this plain from the south and had carried the only bridge over the fast-flowing river virtually by a *coup de main*. In fact, the Cubans had tried to blow it under Delville's nose but they did not succeed.

Rushing for the northern edge of the plain, Delville's leading armoured cars had run into an ambush while negotiating the twisting road to the top of the escarpment. He lost two of his cars and the others pulled back under heavy fire. His mortar platoon, by force of circumstances, had to come into action quickly within sight of a well-dug-in and camouflaged enemy in order to produce sufficient covering fire for the leading elements to withdraw. The result was accurate and effective counter-bombardment fire by FAPLA on the mortar base plate positions. The whole platoon was put out of action with something like 18 casualties, of which one eventually died.

The same little platoon leader who did such a splendid job at Catengue distinguished himself by carrying wounded troops out of the enemy mortar fire in spite of being wounded himself. He was assisted by Piet, an NCO, and Delville's engineer commander. Both were subsequently awarded the Honoris Crux.

Meanwhile we passed Jock's company, which had been called up from Sá da Bandeira to Lobito, without my knowledge, where they were holding a T-junction on the main road to Nova Lisboa and the turn-off to Novo Redondo.

His company had refused to move further north as they were now, according to them, in a "foreign" country for which they felt no affinity, let alone an obligation to shed their blood just to enhance Chipenda's chances to become president one day.

A similar feeling was running through the rest of the unit and although there was no question of another mutiny in the offing, I had decided to pre-empt any action on their part by getting Chipenda to come and talk to them. We were therefore due to meet Chipenda at an airstrip some ten kilometres south of where Delville was having a rather harrowing time.

So when the mango hit the fan for Alpha, I was more inclined to ignore Chipenda's scheduled visit and to push on to a position from where we could assist Delville and his Bushmen.

This was not to be, however, and we pulled into the airstrip as the last Dakota with casualties climbed away over the Atlantic to turn south for SWA and the Republic.

Chipenda's Dakota came in from the east and landed. Chipenda in his usual floral shirt and slacks got out, his well-fed face beaming and giving the FNLA thumbs-up sign. Roars of approval echoed from the assembled troops "FNLA OYEZ! FNLA OYEZ! Chipenda OYEZ!" et cetera. The great guerrilla leader, formerly military commander of FAPLA, raised his farms and launched into a passionate speech.

According to Deaz, one of the Portuguese standing next to me and Frank, he was telling them all about a serpent which had to be killed before Angola would be free. We had been busy with the tail up till then, but the head of the serpent was still in Luanda and that was where we would finally grind the serpent into the dust.

So it was "Luanda here we come!" The troops were impressed, or so I thought, and they cheered Chipenda in answer to his own exultant "FNLA OYEZ!" at the end of his speech.

But suddenly the parade disintegrated as Chipenda made his way to the Dakota to fly him back to Serpa Pinto, the ex-governor's palace, his whisky and his girls. He was harassed from all sides by excited troops not entirely satisfied with his explanation as to why the war had to be fought in what they considered to be a foreign country.

Chipenda, being an astute survivor, backed off, smiling and waving his hands at all and sundry while the enquiries turned into shouts, and I thought, not being a speaker of Portuguese, downright insults judging by fists being shaken in Chipenda's face.

For the moment we stood there perplexed by developments. A manageable, if rather reluctant, body of troops had become within minutes a howling, belligerent mob. I was left with the baby as Chipenda's Dakota lifted off over the Atlantic to turn eastwards towards Serpa Pinto.

All around me was a hotly gesticulating and angry mob of troops shouting at one another and at their erstwhile comman-dantes, the white South Africans being interested – but also very worried – spectators.

To the north 25-pounder guns were booming as they were pounding away at the FAPLA positions. Delville could do with our help at that very moment and I had a rapidly disintegrating unit on my hands.

"Mount!" I shouted. That was all the reaction I could think of at the time. The call was rapidly taken up by my company commanders, platoon leaders and the ex-commandante platoon sergeants. Without further ado, the troops gathered their kit and climbed into their trucks, not even a flicker of resistance to my order.

They knew full well that we were about to drive to the sound of the guns, but they did not seem to mind. What I thought was a mob had, in fact, become a fully disciplined unit over the last few weeks. They were just venting their anger at Chipenda and his comrades. It was as if Chipenda's visit and speech finally purged them of the last vestiges of their loyalty to Angolan politicians who, on the whole, were opportunists, especially Chipenda. With their display of anger they had sworn off their allegiance to FNLA leaders.

From that moment on their leaders would be the white South Africans, for better or for worse. They were now South African soldiers fighting for whichever objectives the South Africans were fighting for.

Never again did I hear any discussions about the whys and wherefores of the war. Doggedly, stoically they carried out orders as we gave them. Chipenda's name was never again mentioned, except in derision by some, probably in sadness by others.

They still did not like UNITA, however, and they assured me on numerous occasions that there was no difference between SWAPO and UNITA which, at the time, was not so far-fetched. There was a kernel of truth in their allegations.

On the way we picked up a frightened FAPLA who had been overtaken by events and was making his way north along the coast. Thirst and hunger got the better of him, however, and he made for the main road where he surrendered by lying in a ditch, next to the road. Very hesitantly he stuck his hands in the air every time a vehicle passed.

We were the first to spot him. According to him quite a large number of disorientated FAPLA troops were slowly drifting northwards from the heavy fighting in Benguela and their rapid evacuation of Lobito.

So we tightened up our security just in case some FAPLA had regained their courage and had decided to spring an ambush on us.

I left my battalion just south of the fighting and proceeded to Delville's command post, which I found on a knoll overlooking the plain at his feet.

Less than a kilometre ahead was the bridge he had taken, with some boulders lying on the roadway. The Cubans had unsuccessfully tried to cave in the adjacent cliff face onto the southern approaches to the bridge. The river was a raging torrent, swollen with the run-off from the seasonal rains.

Having arrived at the observation post, I soon took the appropriate steps to get some cover for myself as Delville could get distinctly unfriendly to people strolling around his domain.

Smokey, the commander of the 25-pounders, had just joined us with his guns. He was as excited as a puppy with ten tails at the chance of using his guns in anger. Unfortunately for him, Delville himself was an old gunner and he was obviously enjoying the opportunity to fire the 25-pounders for the first time at an enemy since the Second World War.

So the old gunner and the young gunner were driving the sharp end of the artillery support, both smiling from ear to ear while a short distance to the rear the troops of guns were cracking away as they hurled very lethal airburst shells overhead towards FAPLA.

Down in the valley FAPLA shells were marching up and down on or near the beach on our left. They were evidently suspecting a left-flanking manoeuvre by Delville's Bushmen.

Meanwhile the 25-pounders were scattering red-hot steel spliners from airbursts 30 ft above ground, on the opposite crest, on the unprotected heads and bodies of FAPLA troops in their shallow open trenches.

I badly wanted to get in on the scene and suggested to Corky that I should take my troops through the very broken terrain on our right, cross the river somehow and fall on FAPLA's left wing with a violent and, hopefully, well-executed night attack. Corky just looked at me and said nothing. The river, which I had not yet seen properly, explained Corky's lack of enthusiasm. When I finally clapped eyes on the river, I saw a rugged gorge, hundreds of feet deep with vertical sides and a raging mass of brown water between its banks.

The bridge could not be crossed because it was under fire and also, right in the open, forming a perfect and lethal bottleneck for our own troops.

Finally FAPLA's shelling started to die down and eventually it stopped. Careful prods by armoured car patrols proved that FAPLA had evacuated the high ground to the north of the plain. It also produced clear evidence that the airburst shells produced a very high percentage of casualties among FAPLA. The tar road and adjacent areas were covered in shell splinters, gaps being torn out of the tar, splashes of blood on the road surface and bloody bandages littering the scene.

As the sun was going down, Delville's troops consolidated their positions. It would be our turn the next morning to push our way into Novo Redondo through a stretch of hilly country just south of the town.

According to Dries, FAPLA was occupying some extremely strong positions, particularly on a very high and dominating feature to the west of the main road. They also had some fifteen 82 mm mortars and some Stalin Organs at their disposal, apart, of course, from the numerous machine guns, B-10s and other recoilless guns and rifles.

I was in no state of mind, therefore, to rush things and I decided to start my attack from a start line behind Delville's line of forward troops. This meant that my attack would move in with troops and armoured cars fully deployed over a distance of some five kilometres.

Smokey's artillery was at my disposal and I decided to have their fire on call, the primary target being the dominating feature west of the road.

We kicked off at first light the next morning with one company to the left and another to the right of the road, armoured cars following behind the infantry and moving from firing position to firing position.

Smokey and I sat on a knoll from where we could view the proceedings, rather like Wellington at Waterloo. This was the first time I actually viewed my own attacks from a distance and it looked very impressive.

Well-drilled and well-armed infantry were moving in a thin line, not red but camouflaged, well spread out, acting like professionals, through the scrub and bush on both sides of the tar road. Behind them followed the equally well-deployed troops of the reserve company.

Armoured cars moved smoothly in bounds from fire position to fire position where they stopped with their 90 mm guns pointing menacingly at what we presumed to be the main FAPLA defensive positions.

I was sipping a mug of coffee while lost in admiration at the war-like tableau at my feet when Corky turned up at my command post. Proudly I swept my arm over the scene below. "That is how it should be done," I explained. Corky however showed no sign that he was impressed. Instead he wanted me to speed up the advance. "We are wasting time," he said.

"What? With all those FAPLAs and Cubans sitting on that hill over there? No way. Delville got a bloody nose yesterday and I have no intention of getting one today. Besides, I am doing it according to the book, probably for the first time, and it looks very good to me."

I was adamant. The process would not be stopped or changed until we had cleared the FAPLA positions in classical style. Corky kept quiet and watched developments below.

So far there was a deathly silence. The hill opposite looked particularly peaceful and my infantry was already steadily moving up the sides, heading for the summit. Smokey watched for just the slightest sign of enemy movement or reaction so that he could let his guns loose to play their airburst over the skyline and beyond.

No sign or movement came and the infantry slowly disappeared out of sight.

"I told you there would be nothing there. You could have moved faster." This from Corky as he made his way back to his vehicle and his headquarters. I got into my Land Cruiser and sped towards where my troops had disappeared, cursing Dries all the way.

Certainly, if FAPLA had been there it would have been a beautiful scrap and I was almost disappointed that we missed out on this one after all the preparations we went through to ensure success.

So it was back to playing Rommel again, instead of Montgomery, hitting the enemy as soon as we made contact without going through the tortuous preparations of mounting deliberate assaults.

I hastened up to Connie's company and told them to rush through the centre of Novo Redondo, without taking any notice of any FAPLA ensconced in the buildings facing the main road, and to take the high ground beyond with a *coup-de-main*-type operation. He had two troops of armoured cars to support him.

Jack would follow up with his company and clear the town itself in the wake of Connie's troops.

Smokey would stay with me and would get his artillery to engage any targets on the high ground beyond, which may interfere with Connie's advance.

Once more we had a beautiful view of the battlefield, below our feet, from a high hill on which there was also a rather prominent radio mast.

Novo Redondo is probably one of the most picturesque towns on the Angolan coast. Most of it was squeezed in between the beach fringed with palm trees, on our left, and the main road leading to the north across a muddy river raging with flood waters. Beyond the river there were some fields, obviously under irrigation, for a distance of about two or three kilometres after which the tar road turned abruptly to the right to wind its way to the top of the escarpment.

The winding road to the top, at that moment, was clogged with fleeing FAPLA traffic. A gleam came to Smokey's eyes and he started to play his artillery, firing airburst over the fleeing columns.

How nice it was to make war from a distance, instead of close up with the enemy, which had been our lot up till then before they gave us our artillery.

Vehicles caught fire, some were abandoned and some FAPLA scampered into the bushes. Soon the road beyond Novo Redondo was deserted.

Meanwhile Connie's men were racing through the town, meeting with wildly cheering schoolchildren and no resistance. It seemed as if the Lobito scene would be repeated.

Frank came up to my OP and I therefore felt free to join Connie as he was approaching the high ground to the north. Just as I left the OP, a Stalin Organ opened fire opposite. I was well on my way down to the main road when the first rockets exploded around Frank's ears on the position I had just vacated. Frank was certainly not amused, mainly because the OP I had selected was so obvious, even to the dimmest FAPLA commander.

I caught up with the leading armoured cars and we proceeded Rommel fashion, as Delville did the previous day south of the town, up the steeply climbing road to the top.

We ran into an ambush in the first cutting we came to. There was an almighty bang as a small suicide group let fly with an RPG-7 at the leading armoured car. Luckily they missed. This was followed by a louder bang from one of the 90 mms and I valiantly dismounted from my vehicle to clear the position with some nearby infantry.

We found two dead FAPLA behind a small wall of stones, with their RPG-7 strangely intact. They were probably killed by the blast only of the 90 mm shell. It had landed just in front of their faces on the other side of their flimsy wall.

We emptied their pockets quickly of all escudos so that we could pay for fresh food later on and looked around for more signs of FAPLA. There were none and I returned to my Land Cruiser.

It had a flat wheel, the spare was also flat, and I was sitting in a cutting overlooked by menacingly high ground beyond. So with a degree of some anxiety, I summoned Frank from his OP to bring up his own spare wheel. He joined me laughing his head off at my predicament, but soon the wheel was fixed. I was mobile again and quickly joined the leading troops.

On top of the escarpment we had a short, sharp engagement after which Connie's infantry cleared out the thick bush in professional style. We found several dead FAPLA and one wounded female soldier who put up a great struggle not to be evacuated. She must have thought that she was about to be raped by my troops, whether wounded or not.

We also found the usual heaps of camouflaged uniform, some of them covered in blood, as FAPLA hastily discarded all evidence that they were soldiers. This was a normal proceeding we had met up with earlier in the campaign and would create problems later on as many of them disappeared among the local population up in the mountains to the east.

Jack had cleared the town and he informed me that he had found the ideal place for our headquarters.

Leaving Connie to consolidate on the high ground I made my way via the cotton factory below, where Corky was already establishing his headquarters.

Jack certainly selected the most imposing structure he could find as the abode for Bravo Group headquarters. It was a huge building with a well-designed ground floor on top of which there sat two separate houses on both sides of a roof garden decorated with potted palms, shrubs and flowers.

Below the roof garden, at the rear of the building, was a driveway leading up to the main steps, flanked by tropical gardens.

In one corner of the main house there was a tower with a small room at the top from where the whole town, the hills to the north, and the fishing fleet swaying at anchor in the bay could be viewed.

The scenery was superb with an old Catholic Church diagonally across from us and a long sweeping beach, fringed with palm trees directly below. The Atlantic surf was breaking in long white rollers all along the crescent of the bay.

A short wooden jetty reached out towards the anchored fishing fleet. The first fishermen were already making their way towards us, laden with freshly caught crayfish for sale. This was going to be paradise.

Frank and I inspected the house and we found that it was well and truly stocked with old English antique furniture, or so our medical doctor assured us. He was an antique connoisseur of some renown from Cape Town.

The place had only just been vacated, judging by the signs of hasty departure. It was not long before a very angry elderly Portuguese couple were mounting the steps to the roof garden where I was in the process of cleaning my rifle after the morning's excitement.

According to Paul they were complaining very strongly that we were illegally occupying the premises. They kept on referring to the law of the land which would get us for breaking in and entering unlawfully. They generally carried on using this tack, shaking their fingers at me, working themselves up to a near tantrum and giving Paul scarcely a chance to translate.

In the end I lost my patience. I had just finished assembling my cleaned rifle, which I did while they were still frothing at the mouth at our presumption at moving in without anybody's permission.

"I am the law in this place now, so get out!" I said while working the working parts of my rifle backwards and forwards to test its smooth functioning, a normal drill every time one re-assembles a rifle.

The effect was electric. They nearly fell over themselves in their haste to get away from a madman who was quite prepared to shoot them. They rushed down the steps, out into the street and around the corner as fast as their elderly legs could carry them.

I was astonished at their reaction but shrugged it off. Good riddance, I thought, and no harm done in spreading the word that the new occupants of the "pink house", as we called it, were a little crazy.

Later on it transpired that the previous occupant had been the governor, under Portuguese rule, of Novo Redondo Province. He was also the owner of the fishing fleet in the bay, two cotton farms and several cocoa farms inland. The man was a multi-millionaire and therefore quite readily changed sides when FAPLA took over Novo Redondo after the Portuguese departure. After all, he wanted to protect his interests and was quite happy to serve under a Marxist government as long as they left him alone to enlarge his piles of escudos.

He no doubt thought that his day of reckoning had arrived when my troops, in the name of FNLA, so suddenly and violently appeared on the scene from the south. He remembered that the local population were mostly FNLA supporters and he therefore "gapped it" in such a hurry that he scarcely had time to pack a suitcase.

In due course his personal servant arrived and proceeded to clear up the place as if nothing had changed. He even took over our washing and soon we were wearing crackling fresh camouflaged uniforms, nicely starched and ironed.

The old boy was quite ancient and also quite amiable. I am sure he had no inkling of what all the fuss, and the war, was about.

Frank discovered some beautiful sets of medals, each with a very pretty ribbon, in the ex-governor's office. There were three sets of 11 each.

I invited Delville and his headquarters to a dinner in my palace and solemnly presented each of them, and each of my officers, with the "Angolan Freedom Medal", the "Catengue Star" and the "Angolan Campaign" medal. The next day we would have a briefing by the Brigadier and I requested all to wear their medals when attending orders which would be in my "house".

The next morning it was a perplexed Brigadier and Colonel Corky who viewed a throng of well-decorated officers in crisp, clean camouflaged fatigues from across the table. Every time we moved our proud chests, the medals clanged together in a very satisfying manner. If Toon had only shaved off his wildly unkempt red beard, the picture would have been perfect enough to be the subject of a very distinguished photograph in *Time* magazine. "South African war heroes gathered together for orders by their war leader, somewhere deep in Angola." That certainly would have rocked our people back home.

"Where did you get those gongs?" asked the Brigadier.

"Well, Chipenda was here early this morning and he had an impromptu medal parade," I said.

"Why didn't I know about it?" asked Corky, viewing the display on our chests with some envy.

"It happened so quickly that I had no time to inform you. He left straight after the parade."

"What are the medals for?" asked the Brigadier.

I explained the significance of each. The ribbons particularly looked impressive, just like real medal ribbons from the Second World War.

We carried on with the briefing, the gist of which was that we had to look for a way to cross the Queve River to the north, either towards Porto Amboim along the coast or from Conda towards Gabela.

On a map the terrain looked formidable with the biggest river yet encountered and rugged mountains inland. Also the rainy season had started in all earnest. Inland, in the valleys, the going would be muddy and soft.

Afterwards we had tea and cake to round off the proceedings, more exactly, fire buckets with army tea and some dog biscuits. In our rather pleasant, elegant surroundings one had to stick to the niceties of civilisation, however. Corky and the Brigadier now had the opportunity to examine our medals more closely, and I am afraid, the joke was on them.

The ex-governor probably had something to do with second league soccer in Angola and Novo Redondo seemed to have won the cup three years in a row. For each year 11 different medals with different coloured ribbons were struck. These were the impressive medals we were sporting on our chests.

We spent the rest of the day preparing for our respective advances further northwards, my group towards Porto Amboim and Delville's towards Gabela. The preparations also included several dips in the Atlantic and lying on the beach soaking up the hot sun.

Jack had meanwhile moved out his company to high ground at a crossroads some ten kilometres north-east of Novo Redondo, thus blocking any advance by FAPLA from either Cabela or Porto Amboim.

Connie was still spread out on the high ground to the north and blocking any approach along the coast, more particularly along the beach.

Grobbie was in reserve with his company at the cotton mill also protecting the brigade headquarters and the airfield.

The next morning I moved out at about 0800 hours for an assault crossing of the Queve River and also to take Porto Amboim before the day was over.

Unfortunately, I had no bridging equipment to cross the

Queve at the vicinity of its mouth if the bridge was found to be blown. Rumours in town had it that the bridge had been blown the night after our arrival in Novo Redondo.

Delville disappeared to the east into the mountains and into the mud of the inland rainy season. We would not see him or hear of him for three days. Corky almost gave Delville and his whole battle group up as lost for good on the third day. I had already flung two patrols – consisting of a platoon of infantry and a troop of armoured cars each – after the Bushmen to try and make contact only for my troops to disappear as mysteriously as Delville and his men did. Evidently a huge FAPLA monster was chewing them up somewhere beyond the mountain passes on our right flank.

But to get back to our imitation of a Rommel advance towards Porto Amboim.

We left in great order, the battle group stringing along at least ten kilometres long on the road to the north and looking very impressive.

Somewhere to the rear Smokey's four 25-pounders were also bouncing along behind their gun tractors, Smokey himself being in his Land Rover right behind my Land Cruiser.

It was a beautiful morning, fresh and cool. The previous night it had rained and we were all in a somewhat light-hearted mood as we barrelled along on top of the escarpment towards the Queve River estuary.

The country was flat along a narrow strip of coast, with the Queve on our right before it bends westwards for the sea just south of Port Ambione. Beyond the Queve, on our right, the hills rose in tier after tier, becoming rugged mountains in the direction of Gabela. To our left we could see the blue Atlantic over the lip of the escarpment. A very narrow beach, which we could not see, was wedged between the cliff face of the escarpment and the surf line.

Cotton fields stretched as far as the eye could see to the north. It was just the start of the rainy season so that the veld alongside was still wearing its drab tawny winter colours. There was very little cover, the bush being very sparse.

The whole battle group therefore stood out like a sore thumb against the background of brown earth and dead grass as it wound its way along the tar road to the north.

Just south of the Queve flood plain, on its westerly course for the sea, I decided to stop the whole column while probing carefully towards the bridge with a troop of armoured cars and a platoon of infantry.

I went with them as I wanted to determine with my own eyes that the bridge was, in fact, blown as rumour in Novo Redondo would have it.

The road passed through a neck between two pimples, the only two hills south of the river, and broke into a flood plain about five kilometres wide towards the bridge in the distance, which lay in the shadow of hulking cliffs just north of the river's main stream.

The cliffs stretched all along our front and were so high that it masked any FAPLA positions from our view. The river was in flood, so we crept along on top of a causeway with swamps and reeds to both sides, which made deployment off the road impossible for armoured cars and for my troop carriers.

The troop carriers were particularly vulnerable as there was no way they could quickly get out of danger if caught on the causeway by FAPLA. They would be sitting ducks. So I stopped Anton and his platoon and proceeded on my own with the armoured cars.

We saw some FAPLA soldiers in the swamps to our left, probably patrols deployed to prevent a night approach, and from the lofty bed of the causeway we opened fire.

They quickly disappeared in the reeds. Ahead we could see the bridge, well and truly destroyed.

Our firing at the FAPLA patrol seemed to signal the opening of proceedings, because very rapidly the swamps on both sides started to sprout numerous gigantic mushrooms of dirty water, mud and smoke. No shells fell on the road.

We therefore very leisurely turned the armoured cars round on the narrow tar surface and made our way back towards the two pimples. FAPLA was shepherding us away from Porto Amboim in no uncertain manner.

While crossing the saddle between the pimples, I could see my battle group spread out, almost in plan form, on both sides of the road as it descended gently from the highest point of the plain to the south.

The descent started at the horizon about ten kilometres away and it finally levelled out just north of the pimples.

From their cliff face top, much higher than we were, FAPLA must have had a marvellous view. They could count every armoured car, troop carrier and gun at their leisure, plot them at their leisure and shoot them up at their leisure.

Because of the previous night's rain, deployment off the road was nearly impossible, except on foot. My men were therefore strung up and down both sides of the road, all of them dismounted and some even brewing up, not taking any notice whatsoever of the shell bursts.

Our progress to Porto Amboim and points further north had, however, been effectively stopped along that particular route, only because we could not bridge the flooding Queve and not so much because of a lack of aggressiveness on our part.

But the "Boers", as FAPLA called us, whether black or white, could not just meekly turn south again. Thus far we have not only fought against an ever-increasing FAPLA resistance but also the dust, sand, flies and mud of Angola. We did not want to bow out with a whimper but rather with a bang.

A defiant gesture was therefore called for so I asked Smokey to come forward. He arrived in his Land Rover with Frank in his Land Cruiser accompanying him.

With Anton's platoon acting as local protection, we ascended the eastern pimple to establish an OP from where Smokey could hammer FAPLA with his guns.

The progress up the hill was slippery and very muddy, the sticky mess building up under our boots, but soon we were at the top from where five Stalin Organ positions could be seen. They were all firing at us in turn and most of the rockets seemed to be aimed at the particular pimple we were standing on.

Our command vehicles left on the road in the saddle also seemed to be a target. Mine collected a bit more shrapnel just after Paul and I had dismounted, and if memory serves me right, Frank and Smokey's drivers were pinned down in a ditch next to their vehicles throughout the engagement.

Smokey proceeded to range with his guns, which incidentally were deployed just east of the road in full view of the enemy.

His first shot was in the air when it was crossing a clearly visible rocket on its way to us, the burning motor betraying its launch with the characteristic red flare which gave it its nick name of the "Red Eye".

"Here she comes!" I shouted and we all ducked into the mud. The rocket exploded about 50 yards to our left in a shower of mud and smoke.

"Repeat!" ordered Smokey as he had lost his first shot when taking cover.

"Shot!" from the guns, followed by time of flight. There stood Smokey with his binoculars firmly clamped to his eyes, expectantly waiting for the tell-tale mushrooming of his own 25-pounder shell. Something seemed to be wrong with the binoculars because he kept on fiddling with the eyepieces.

"Here she comes!" I shouted again and it was a repeat performance by a command group now getting muddy in the process.

The rocket fell short, but once again Smokey was out of luck. "Repeat!" from Smokey.

"Shot!" from the guns. "Time of flight so many seconds."

"Here she comes!" from me and once more we all ducked into the mud.

In between, Smokey fiddled with his binoculars. "Has anyone seen my shot?" he asked hopefully. None of us had.

Eventually Smokey found his first visible ranging shot, just short of the enemy cliff face and probably in the water, judging by the mushroom. He marched his ranging shots onto the first Stalin Organ position and proceeded to plaster it with airburst.

He also found the reason for his difficulty in seeing his shots through his binoculars. Both lenses were well and truly coked in mud and all Smokey could see was utter darkness, not even a sliver of light coming through his lenses.

Every time he ducked, the binoculars dangling around his neck would be pressed deep into the sticky putty that made up most of the pimple we were standing on.

Smokey had taken out three of the Stalin Organ positions when the remaining two decided that for some reason or other the command group on the pimple seemed to be immune to rocket fire.

But they could see the 25-pounders parked plainly in sight and within range next to the road, so they shifted their fire to the gun lines.

Soon we could hear by the sound of the rockets passing overhead that they were not coming towards us but going away to more lucrative targets to the rear.

Looking back, we could see the muddy plain flowering with rocket bursts around the gun lines. It wasn't long before the guns were forced to pack up and withdraw across the skyline to the south. They were out of sight and range of the Stalin Organs but also could not reach them from their new positions.

So that concluded our efforts to find a crossing over the Queve. There was nothing more we could do. I decided to withdraw back to Novo Redondo, but to do so without undue haste. We formed up the whole column, facing south, and very sedately proceeded to withdraw, the command group bringing up the rear.

The rockets followed us spasmodically for a while and then stopped.

We had no casualties, just a little bit of minor damage to the final drive of one of the armoured cars and a few extra holes through my Land Cruiser.

Sources reported that Smokey's outbursts caused quite a bit of havoc on the FAPLA positions. Numerous casualties were evacuated to Porto Amboim for treatment in the hospital there.

So although circumstances forced us to leave the field of battle, we had the better of the enemy as far as casualties and damage to morale were concerned. We left with our tails up, only feeling frustrated that we had no engineer support to make a river crossing possible.

On the way back I dispatched a troop of armoured cars and some infantry to confirm that the bridge on the direct road from Novo Redondo to Gabela, and also the Queve, had in fact been destroyed.

Although all our sources reported that this was the case, none of our troops had actually seen the destroyed bridge. It spanned a very narrow gorge on the Queve and was overlooked, on the Gabela side, by high buttresses and cliff faces. On our side the road descended gradually through a very deep and narrow cutting about a kilometre in length in a straight line to the bridge itself. Luckily there were no FAPLA yet on the far side among the buttresses, as the armoured cars were sitting ducks as they proceeded between the vertical walls of the cutting down to the bridge.

Later on FAPLA would be there in force, which caused some anxious and exciting moments for Delville and his Bushmen.

The bridge was found to be well and truly blown. There was even less chance of crossing the raging torrent at this spot than there was further down. We returned to Novo Redondo and reported to Corky.

A stalemate became a real possibility and everything now hinged on Delville's probe further to the east, that is if something disastrous had not happened to his column, of which there was still no sign.

However, after three days Delville reappeared out of the mountains in the east together with my two patrols which were sent to look for his battle group. They and their vehicles were covered in mud as they had been caught in the full force of the rainy season.

In Angola the rain is much heavier inland than along the coast, which is relatively dry. Consequently, the going is much more difficult, especially off-road where it becomes almost impossible. Delville also had to contend with rugged mountains and rather indifferent mountain passes.

The population also seemed to become more sympathetic to FAPLA the further inland he went.

This made for some rather amusing, always interesting and

at times hairy incidents, which would be an interesting story to tell and inextricably part of the history of 201 Battalion, or Alpha Group as it was known.

Meanwhile I had decided that a light patrol a short distance into the mountains of the interior and along the Queve was necessary, to find hopefully, an overlooked crossing site.

Leading the patrol I set out with Frank's and my Land Cruisers, some infantry and a troop of armoured cars.

We left in bright sunshine and proceeded westwards along quite a good dirt road which entered some hills about ten kilometres to the east. Soon the road became a track and we entered the damp grey blanket of clouds which clothed the higher mountains permanently at this time of the year.

Rain began to fall and we got soaked in our open vehicles. The armoured cars merely closed down and stayed snug and dry.

We passed numerous hamlets and villages where the population stared at us silently and with some hostility. We were obviously not welcome. The spontaneous relief and joy on the faces of the Novo Redondo population, when the town was liberated, were completely absent here.

This could be ascribed to either a virtually complete support for MPLA, which I doubted, or to the fact that a lot of FAPLA had discarded their uniforms, during our attack on Novo Redondo, and were now hiding among the population in the mountains, but also keeping them in line with all sorts of threats against their persons or possessions if they were betrayed.

I prefer the latter explanation because, in my experience of Africa, I have always found that the rural African population are indifferent to the competing ideologies or political parties that make up the political substance of African countries.

They will side with whomever is carrying the gun at the moment, at the same time hoping to stay clear of any confrontation.

Obviously we were just a patrol passing through. It would therefore not do any good at all to welcome the strangers, to even offer guidance, while several FAPLA among them were watching proceedings with their AK rifles safely tucked away under a bush, in the roof of a hut, or elsewhere. The knives would be out to liquidate the sympathisers once we had gone.

At the same time we were very aware of the fact that bands of armed FAPLA troops could still be moving around in the mountains, dressed in civilian attire and therefore more dangerous as they would be more difficult to spot.

It was perfect ambush country and particularly ideal for mines. They had no vehicles using the roads and tracks. Any vehicle blown up therefore would be an FNLA vehicle. The pouring rain favoured the laying of mines as all signs and spoor would be washed away.

Cautiously, therefore, we wound our way through the mountains as if we were driving on eggs with that characteristic tight feeling in one's backside when one expects a mine to go off at any moment.

The country was lush with dripping thick bush and tall trees screening mountainsides and ravines.

Every once in awhile one would break into a small valley to find cocoa plantations and even the odd coffee farm.

We finally reached the Queve River again, winding its way through the wet mountains. At a likely crossing site we were forced to dismount and march through a swamp to take a closer look at the main stream.

I found a place, which seemed practical for troops on foot to cross, but one look at the faces of my accompanying foot patrol quickly disabused me. I had intended to cross over and have a look at the country beyond and I had informed my patrol accordingly. They stared at the raging waters in horror and were adamant that they would not cross that river under any circumstances.

The bare bones of a plan was beginning to form in my mind: to operate on the other side as guerrillas on foot and to ambush the FAPLA communication lines between Gabela and Porto Amboim, eventually infiltrating enough troops to take Porto Amboim itself.

The lines of communication consisted of a tar road and a

narrow gauge railway line, both tortuously winding their respective ways through mountain passes – ideal targets for small groups of infantry.

This was the plan I wanted to sell to Corky. However, I would have to overcome my troops' reluctance to cross a wildly flowing river which was in spate. Perhaps we would have to design a suitable way of doing so with the local means and material available in the absence of any engineer support.

For the moment, we moved further downstream by vehicle to a place where the out-of-date map indicated a drift of some sorts.

We emerged from the mountains into beautiful warm sunshine and we soon dried out.

The cocoa and coffee farms had given way to cotton and citrus and we soon approached a very large citrus estate, beautifully laid out and guarding the site of the drift indicated on the map.

The population also became much more friendly. They gave us assistance in finding the right place. It was quite obvious, however, that no vehicle could pass at that time of the year. No doubt in the dry season it would be feasible, but at that moment a huge wave of brown water was tumbling and foaming over the crossing site.

The road wound along the southern bank of the river and joined the main road at the spot where the bridge, spanning the narrow gorge between Gabela and Novo Redondo, had been blown.

We had every intention of following the road as far down as the bridge, and to return to Novo Redondo along this shorter route.

But the friendly locals warned us in time. FAPLA had, just that morning, begun to take up position in the crags on the north side, possibly as a result of our probe the previous day.

It would therefore be suicide to proceed further, as we would be under fire for several kilometres along our approach to the bridge, and also while making our way back to Novo Redondo through the steep-sided cutting.

We returned the way we came, plunging back into the dull grey cloud and incessant rain of the mountains. The mine and ambush threat would be more real this time. Any guerrilla worth his salt would prepare a hot reception in the event of a return along the same route.

Furthermore, there was only this one route we could follow. So we ran the gauntlet of our own fears and the hostile staring eyes of the bedraggled population as we drove through the wet and miserable villages, fully expecting a violent reception around every bend, or at least a giant "cracker" to go off under one of the wheels of the Land Cruisers or armoured cars.

Nothing happened, fortunately. Sighing with relief, we emerged from the mountains to complete the journey in double-quick time to Novo Redondo.

Corky listened to my ideas, thought it had merit, but also informed me that either my battle group or Delville's would have to move to the central front inland at Cela in the very near future. Whoever stayed behind could carry on along the lines I had suggested.

I was hoping that we would stay and that Delville would have to go.

This, however, was not to be. A few days later I got my marching orders for Cela.

Corky and his headquarters would come along. Delville moved into the pink house and his troops took over the high ground to the north.

We said goodbye for good to probably the nicest little town on the whole Angolan coast.

SIXTEEN
Cela

We left Novo Redondo with all of my battle group and most of Toon's armoured car squadron. The rest stayed behind under Delville's command. His was to be an independent command, and although ostensibly a backwater, since the main thrust was now to be up the centre towards Luanda, he could develop and control the war on his front without undue interference from higher headquarters.

An independent command is always desired by all true soldiers and, while wishing Delville luck, I was a little disappointed that I could not be in his shoes.

Soon another FNLA battalion, under the command of a commandante by the name of Chiote, joined Delville. They did some good work while working with him. This battalion, Chiote included, was destined to become the other half of Bravo Group after the demise of Savannah.

Chiote himself was quite a character. He ruled his men with an iron fist and completely lacked fear in battle. He once executed two of his men, on a parade ground, because they had deserted their trenches on the high ground north of Novo Redondo. He then buried them, each in his own trench, calmly informing his troops that never again would they be capable of leaving their positions to go and gallivant in town while others had to stick it out in the cold and wet of the now fully arrived rainy season!

The whole column moved south in dry weather towards the Lobito-Nova Lisboa road before swinging east and climbing through the hills to the highlands of central Angola.

The weather gradually deteriorated as we proceeded inland, climbing ever higher until it became drizzly and distinctly cool. The fall in temperature was quite unexpected as we were deep inside the tropics.

The coastal bush gave way to more luxuriant vegetation, tall trees and eventually fairly intensively cultivated fields and meadows with fat cattle grazing contentedly in the lush grass.

The population density also increased considerably and we passed through fair-sized towns before stopping for the night at a largish place called Alto Hama. By this time the rain was pelting down. Reconnoitring the town before nightfall to find dry quarters for the troops became a problem.

I was lucky to find a very large fruit-packing shed into which the whole battalion fitted comfortably, with enough wooden fruit boxes to burn for warmth and to dry out their wet clothes.

Toon and I adjourned to a small room on the first floor of the local hotel (which was abandoned) while Zulu headquarters took up the lounge and dining room on the ground floor.

We had dinner by candlelight with Zulu headquarters. Later on Toon, Dries and I adjourned to our room where we proceeded to demolish a demijohn of wine which Dries had managed to lay his hands on. Dries sings rather well. Soon his voice accompanied by the less accomplished voices of Toon and myself, drifted through the dark corridors of the empty hotel and finally down to the lounge where a very tired Zulu headquarters were trying to get some rest.

They were not amused and Dries got it in the neck the next morning.

We headed north and crossed the wide-flowing Queve by a bridge, left miraculously intact, on our way to Cela. Cela was also the headquarters of Foxbat, the battle group fighting up the centre of Angola.

On our arrival there, Zulu headquarters would take Foxbat under its wing, and so with Bravo and Toon's squadron already under command, we would be getting back to the previous strength we had at Novo Redondo. Corky would not be with us much longer. He was due to leave for the Republic after about a week or so of handing over to Blackie, the new commander. He had, however, not yet arrived at Cela.

Changes had also taken place in Foxbat. Eddie had been replaced by George some time previously and Holly, Eddie's second on command, was also about to leave.

We pulled into Cela to be greeted with a crisis situation. Schalkie was the SSO operations, and in the absence of Blackie, was also running the war on the ground. He was obviously glad to see us. I got the impression that we were something like the US Cavalry, just arriving in the nick of time to prevent a full-scale massacre by the Indians.

George had run into very fierce resistance at a place called Ebo on a roundabout route to Gabela which was now lying north-west of us. Gabela still seemed to be the objective for the moment.

George had lost quite a number of armoured cars and a lot of infantry while pushing across a minor river in the face of a heavy FAPLA concentration on high ground north of the crossing.

FAPLA were following up their unexpected success by trying to cut off George's withdrawal. If FAPLA's envelopment was successful, there would be nothing left to stop them from overrunning Cela in very short order as there would be no troops to stop a determined attack.

No wonder Schalkie looked a bit worried, because they were nicely ensconced in what turned out to be a monastery. Maps were displayed against the walls of a proper operations room, there were proper communication facilities, a proper mess, proper rooms to sleep in, a hospital next door with Tony, later to be known as the "Surgeon of Cela," in charge and even a well-equipped LWT.

To vacate all that in a hurry would be impossible. Thank God, we in Zulu Force learnt early on that we had to be fully mobile. It was just a matter of climbing in one's vehicle, starting up and going in whichever direction one was ordered by the powers that be.

Cela also had a very good airfield into which a lot of equipment was flown, by C-130s and C-160s, on a daily basis.

The war had achieved a more South African flavour over the past few weeks or so. In fact, it struck me forcibly that most of the troops around Cela headquarters were white troops and not blacks, although in all fairness, a sizeable force of UNITA, of dubious quality however, was deployed on the high ground to the north of Santa Comba.

Santa Comba was about ten kilometres north of Cela and, in fact, the main town of the area. Cela was just an abandoned mission station.

Schalkie and Corky decided that I had to take up an intermediate position on high ground east of Foxbat to cover George's withdrawal and to hold up FAPLA's advance if they should follow up.

We therefore headed north past Santa Comba without delay, turned west just south of high ground occupied by UNITA and some armoured cars, and took up position facing west, in the direction from which George would appear in due course. We were just short of a fork in the road.

One of the roads leading from the fork was known as the blue route, the other as the green route. I cannot remember which route was which colour, but for the purpose of this narrative we will call the southernmost road the green route and the northern one the blue route.

George was on the green route which crossed the small river, parallel to our delaying position some distance to the right, at a place called Ebo. This was the scene of George's anguish.

The blue route led more directly to Gabela but, from what I could see, through more broken terrain. Therefore, it was less suitable than the green route. I decided to send the usual patrols, consisting of a troop of armoured cars and a platoon of infantry, along both routes for a distance of about ten kilometres where they would take up positions to act as early warning against a FAPLA advance and also to delay them for as long as possible.

For all I knew George might already be overrun by FAPLA in which case we could very soon expect to see a drunk-with-victory FAPLA crowd knocking violently at our front door if we did not act quickly.

We therefore set about deploying our companies, armoured cars and my three-inch mortars and machine guns as effectively as possible, under the cover of our previously deployed forward patrols.

We were nicely dug in when the first movement was spotted on the green route to the west. It was George's 25-pounders pulling back at a fast pace.

They passed us without stopping, followed by the armoured cars and finally by the remains of the infantry. The infantry stopped within our lines. Only then did I realise that they were, in fact, two of the companies we left behind, one in Moçâmedes under Costa (my famous old trigger-happy C Company) and the other one Jock's company, which was now run by Silva. They were a bloody mess with quite a lot of wounded in the trucks.

Silva was in command of the remnants of both. Costa had been severely wounded through both legs and was out of the war for good. He was in one of the trucks and he looked dreadful.

George pulled in briefly, obviously glad to see new faces, and he took his headquarters to an old pig farm further south. I took the remains of my two companies back under my command and sat down with Silva to discuss their future.

Silva told me the bloody story of my old Charlie Company and my heart bled for them.

Evidently they crossed the river at Ebo ahead of the armoured cars and spread out to advance further, unaware of the fact that the high ground to their left was teeming with FAPLA, mostly Cubans.

When they were right out in the open, and unable to fall back, FAPLA opened with murderous automatic, mortar and other shell fire, quickly cutting down the whole company, including the company commander.

Silva, luckily, was still on the other side of the river and he covered the withdrawal of the remnants of C Company.

Meanwhile the armoured cars were having their own problems, coming under accurate anti-tank fire and getting stuck in the mud when trying to manoeuvre their way out of danger. I believe that something like seven armoured cars were knocked out.

Charlie's casualties were between 80 and 90 killed or wounded. Most of the wounded could not get away and were killed, on the spot, by the Cubans and by FAPLA troops. Costa, luckily, escaped these cold-blooded executions, but had to crawl back several kilometres to get out of danger. Because of his wounds he was unable to walk.

I did not expect to get my companies back in such a state; in fact, I had thought that they were still doing their thing in Moçâmedes, in the case of Costa's company, and at the crossroads on the Nova Lisboa-Lobito road, in the case of Jock's company.

I was even unaware of the fact that Jock had gone home. I confirmed Silva in his position as company commander, joined the remnants of Charlie Company to his company and renamed it Delta Company.

I withdrew the company for recuperation and reorganisation to a cheese factory some distance to the south. They also had to act as a reserve for the moment.

Meanwhile we waited for FAPLA, but they did not put in an appearance. They were obviously not so hot in the "advance-to-contact" bit as they were, during this isolated instance, in the defensive role at Ebo.

We stayed the night and by the next morning Zulu headquarters had decided to reorganise the whole show.

Toon and all his armoured cars went to George. So did Connie and his A Company. George was to advance along the blue route this time, towards Gabela.

I was to take over two of the armoured car troops from George and to take up another intermediate position further south from our present positions. We also had to man a combat outpost line on high ground some five kilometres south of a bridge called Bridge Fourteen, to be made famous by George's escapades some weeks later.

Bridge Fourteen was on the direct route to Quibala and Luanda in the north. I was also to find out whether Bridge Fourteen was demolished or not.

Connie left with his company up the blue route. So did Toon with his cars.

Meanwhile it was becoming obvious to me that my troops were getting battle weary. Over the previous two weeks or so our fighting was not too violent or too frequent. Before that, however, we had up to five contacts a day, each day bringing its own quota of fear and danger. One's nervous system can only stand so much and will eventually crack if the pressure of fear remains constant over an extended period of time. The real danger lies in driving one's men too far, beyond the point of no return, in which case the damage done may be irreparable.

Even while we were taking up our new positions, in the usual mud and constant rain, 122 mm rockets were coming over from time to time from the vicinity of Catofe, just north of Bridge Fourteen.

I remember one incident when I visited my reconstituted Delta Company at the cheese factory. Rockets were mushrooming in the plain around us while I talked to Silva. The UNITA troops, as usual, were streaming past us back from their positions on the right of my combat outpost line. They always withdrew as soon as the enemy artillery opened up, to return later in the day when FAPLA had let up with their bombardment.

My troops appeared completely oblivious of the rockets. Not one of them bothered to dig in. They stared at UNITA with lacklustre eyes, not even bothering to pass the normal witty and cutting comments on UNITA's fighting capability. This, to me, was a sure sign of battle fatigue in the company.

Deeply moved and deeply perturbed, I went to look up my company commanders to confer with them. They confirmed my suspicions.

While the troops would go on almost indefinitely, their fighting would become less and less effective. If we had to assault a strong FAPLA position, I would probably have a lot of casualties, mostly through sheer indifference and blunted reflexes.

In spite of heavy fighting, we had, throughout the campaign, very few desertions. One could have expected a lot, particularly as it was not too difficult to disappear among the local population.

At Cela I had a few who decided to head south, away from the enemy. They were not black troops but white Portuguese, and I am sad to say, one South African. He was, thank goodness, not from my unit but got loosely attached to D Company by accident rather than design.

The rest of the soldiers bore their lot stoically. That made me all the more determined to fight to get them back to a rest area. They had proved to be extremely loyal under very adverse conditions and deserved my loyalty and the loyalty of all their commanders.

The sickness rate also increased, another sure sign of battle fatigue. Many went down with malaria. The first white platoon leader to go was Anton, followed by Nel and others. Nel had been with me from the start at M'pupa.

Then Jack got malaria and was evacuated. Good old Jack. Quick and unafraid in battle but always, bless him all the same, so reluctant to talk to me on his radio. Every time he was way ahead of his radio operator, who more often than not had taken cover, with the radio, to stare perplexedly at the thing from which there permanently seemed to issue a stream of swear words as I tried to get Jack to talk to me.

With a heavy heart I said goodbye to Jack and I gave his company to James.

Blackie had arrived and he and I were driving through my delaying position when I noticed a very rusty-looking Vickers machine gun peeking around a telegraph pole, a very isolated and very obvious position in which to place a machine gun and therefore an idiotic place for deploying it. I spoke to the Vickers platoon leader, the one who had replaced Fingers, and I chewed him out particularly about the state of the gun.

He had shown very little interest in his platoon up until then. When he started ranting about the uselessness of the black troops, I lost my temper, especially after the ordeals they had gone through which the new machine-gun commander had not.

The Vickers platoon always had been sharp under Fingers' guidance and I had gained a lot of respect for their fighting ability, indeed for the fighting ability of all my black troops.

I told him he was a useless machine-gun platoon leader and

promptly relieved him of his command. All he had achieved was to break down the morale of my Vickers platoon.

It was then necessary to attach sections of the Vickers platoon permanently to each company, but in the absence of a suitable platoon leader, it was preferable that way.

Bridge Fourteen still had to be reconnoitred. I gave the task to Danny with his platoon, and gave him four armoured cars in support, to work up to a feature, known by then as Top Hat, and ascertain whether the bridge had been blown, whether FAPLA was dug in on the other side and whether a crossing on foot or vehicle would be feasible.

Top Hat was a rather high hill west of the main road to Luanda. The road bends around the foot of Top Hat shortly before crossing the river at Bridge Fourteen. The bridge was therefore obscured from our view, at the combat outpost line, by the slopes of the hill.

Danny set off gamely during the morning with his patrol. I arrived at the outpost line later in the day, but just in time to hear a tremendous scrap developing around the bottom slopes of Top Hat.

Danny was in trouble and I had visions of his platoon and the armoured cars being cut to pieces.

Then I saw two cars dashing back at top speed from the direction of the bridge. My fears seemed to be confirmed especially when I gathered, through the radio of the troop leader on the outpost line, that Danny had been attacked by a large FAPLA force.

What worried me most was that Danny and his infantry were being left in the lurch by the rapidly retreating armoured cars. By this time it was apparent that only two cars, instead of the four from the whole troop, went with Danny in the first place.

I dashed to my Land Rover in the cutting and drove towards the armoured cars in order to stop them. I intended to turn them round so that we could get Danny and his men out of trouble.

They stopped but refused to go back, citing the heavy FAPLA fire at Top Hat which would knock them out. The troop leader pointed out that we were even then under 122 mm rocket fire, as shells were bursting all around us.

We certainly were under heavy fire, but not rocket fire – mortar fire. This was a lot more dangerous than rocket fire. I did not enlighten him, however, as he was already far too skittish for my liking.

Fortunately, Danny and his crew put in an appearance before I had to employ harsher methods to convince the armoured car commander to turn back to Top Hat. Danny and his men therefore rode the last few kilometres on the armoured cars as they dashed through the mortar fire back to the outpost line.

Danny's story was remarkable.

He arrived with his patrol at Top Hat where he decided to leave all his men, and the cars, while he went ahead on foot, on his own, to reconnoitre the bridge.

Unbeknown to him, he passed through a very strong FAPLA position on Top Hat's slopes from where they watched Danny with eagle and expectant eyes as he marched his solitary way to his doom at the bridge.

Danny turned the corner, at the bridge, saw that it was blown and also that there were three Cubans standing around what appeared to be a 14,5 anti-aircraft gun on the far side of the river. He promptly shot two of them, after which all hell broke loose as all sorts of weapons opened up on him from the far side.

So he decided to beat a hasty retreat back to his patrol, along the same route that he had come. He ran slap-bang into the FAPLA on the slopes of Top Hat who had a glorious view of a speeding little man thumping the tar road within metres past their positions. They opened up with relish, but somehow it did not quite work out the way they had planned.

Danny told me the story in his own inimitable Portuguese way.

"Colonel, I run and I go tat tat tat tat – and I run and I go tat tat tat tat – and I run and I go tat tat tat tat – and suddenly the shooting it stops; no more FAPLA." He smiled from ear to ear. Danny claimed to have shot two Cubans. He did not claim more.

But as luck would have it, FAPLA on Top Hat had caught two of Danny's men when they tried to round up some cattle while Danny was on his way to the bridge.

Both were kept separately as prisoners at Catofe, one by Cubans and the other by FAPLA, and both escaped separately with a two-day interval between the escapes.

While we debriefed them, it transpired that Danny had shot a total of 11 – two Cubans and nine FAPLA – the latter while dashing through the ambush on Top Hat.

Danny was evidently the talk of the town in Catofe and both escapees overheard the troops discussing the incident while they were having a booze-up the night after it happened.

Later I recommended Danny for the Honoris Crux and I am happy to say that it was approved: the first Portuguese, from the former Portuguese Colonies, in the South African Army to receive this decoration. The chunky Danny had been a famous elephant poacher in Mozambique who also ran his own group of black Frelimo hunters very successfully indeed.

Meanwhile Corky felt happy that he was leaving us in Blackie's good hands. He therefore decided to make his way southwards and back to "civilisation".

He invited Toon, myself, and some of the other old hands to a bit of a party with him and his staff.

There was not much left of Corky's headquarters. Willie had gone on long ago to command Force X-Ray, pushing eastwards along the Benguela railway line. Dries was still around and so were some of the Portuguese members of his staff. All the others had gone home.

So, under fairly subdued circumstances, we started to polish off some beers and some whisky.

Where Corky got the booze from was a mystery, as we hardly ever saw the stuff. In fact, a whole C-160 load of beer had disappeared somewhere along the line while on its way to the fighting troops at Cela. Whisky was just beginning to trickle through and was, in fact, supposed to be an issue to officers.

Well, I personally never received a bottle and we sometimes had to make do with an Angolan whisky which was, believe it or not, called "Shell" whisky. It also tasted more like petrol than whisky. Presumably the "distillery" filled their bottles at the refinery in Luanda.

In the usual South African fashion we had a "braai" and everybody present seemed to enjoy a chance to get out of the incessant rain and into more congenial company and surroundings. It was not long before we all started reminiscing and, of course, to compare our splendid dash up the west coast with the more cautious advance of Foxbat up the centre.

Being conceited, slightly inebriated soldiers, we soon concluded that we formed the most intrepid battle-wise and aggressive force of all the troops fighting in Angola and that they all could profitably learn from our experience and listen to our wise words on the subject of war.

The party turned a bit maudlin towards the end and I decided that our intrepid commander could not leave Zulu without a suitable gesture from our side.

I fished my medals, that is the Catengue Star, the Angolan Freedom Medal and the Angolan Campaign Medal, out of my pocket and ceremoniously pinned them on Corky's broad chest. To complete the ceremony, I kissed him on both cheeks continental style (after all, we were fighting among a people steeped in Portuguese tradition) and solemnly shook his hand in congratulations.

Corky was a proud man. I even fancied a slight mistiness in his eyes, but it could also have been the whisky or the smoke from the fire.

He presumably made a speech, although I cannot remember it, but he walked away with three clanking medals on his chest won by the Novo Redondo second-league soccer team. All the same, these medals may even become collector's items one day, in view of the circumstances under which they were won.

Corky will still have his collection, knowing him as well as I do, and I am minus mine. But I could not have given it to a better man, because Corky really kept the show together, with two difficult customers like Delville and Breytenbach under his command.

He was also the driving force, pushing us hard, sometimes too hard for my liking. On more than one occasion I felt like telling him to "get stuffed".

It is a matter of fact, however, that Zulu Force advanced something like 90 kilometres a day against an enemy who sometimes managed to get their act together, although they were somewhat scrappy in their efforts most of the time.

The reason why FAPLA could not stop us was not our fire superiority, which, in any case was a debatable point, but because they were always put off-balance by the speed at which we advanced. They never had time to dig in and prepare sufficiently well to stop us before, once again, we would suddenly appear to hit them for a six.

Unfortunately, the situation became a stalemate for reasons already discussed. At Cela we found ourselves in a plodding war, almost solely because of the terrain – especially because of the mud which restricted the movement of armoured cars off the main roads.

Ahead there also lay the Cuanza River between us and Luanda. It is the biggest river in Angola. The bridge over this river had been blown, which would mean a major engineering effort in order to cross a very wide, furiously flowing, rain-swollen body of water. But we had no bridging equipment.

The Brigadier and I discussed the stalemate problem. He felt that we should work some flexibility into the situation again.

As a result it was decided that I should form a force that would operate on their feet off the roads, in the thick bush, mountains and mud, in guerrilla fashion behind enemy lines. We would blow up selected bridges on their lateral communications, ambush convoys and attack gun lines and headquarter areas.

My men, I thought, could come from some of the Reconnaissance Commando teams, from an understrength parachute company and from selected black soldiers from my own unit.

Although I managed to get one patrol started off on a mission, unsuccessfully as it turned out to be, the idea never really got off the ground. It died completely after I left Angola.

Meanwhile I visited George on the blue route from time to time in order to get acquainted with the terrain and to see how Connie and his A Company were shaping.

We had brought up 140 mm guns with which to tackle the Stalin Organs because it had a longer range than the 25-pounders. It could also shoot further than the 122 mm Red Eye rockets.

FAPLA, however, replied with 122 mm guns which could outrange our 140 mm guns.

So George was under fire from these guns, on the blue route, to which he could not reply effectively with his own guns.

On one occasion I found Foxbat on the muddy track in the vicinity of a huge coffee plantation with Connie's company establishing a bridge head on the other side of a fast-flowing stream. Connie had picked his way through an unmarked minefield and was, in fact, lucky to be alive, having nearly set one off with his Land Rover.

He came to me somewhat hesitant but also with emotion showing in his face. "The troops are tired," he said. "They will keep on fighting until we tell them to stop, but it is unfair to drive them so hard."

I looked at them lying in the mud where they had dug in to escape FAPLA's artillery fire. FAPLA was, in fact, using airburst for the first time.

"The troops asked for just three weeks' leave and they will be back to chase FAPLA right out of Angola," Connie continued.

I had already mentioned to the Brigadier that my troops were tired and that we must pull back for rest and recuperation. He agreed that the whites could be replaced, but not the blacks as there were no black replacements.

I therefore decided that we all had to stay, whites and blacks, and I informed the Brigadier accordingly.

It was not long, however, before young white second lieutenants arrived straight from the Infantry School to replace my old experienced platoon leaders.

I refused to accept them, except where a platoon leader was evacuated because of sickness. The remaining company commanders and platoon leaders in Bravo Group refused to budge in any case. They wanted to stay with their troops until the end, come hell or high water.

For me it was the most emotional and heart-warming experience of the whole war. My black troops were looking at us, as their leaders, not only to lead in battle but also to look after their welfare.

They, after all, were FNLA and not even remotely South African. But their own leader, Chipenda, had left them in the lurch. He was, in fact, already winging his way to Europe, having spotted the danger signs early on that the South Africans were on the point of withdrawing from Angola.

This left us, the white South Africans, carrying the can and as a body, my white leaders decided to throw in their lot with the blacks.

Over the months we had come to know our troops and to respect their fighting ability. They had done our bidding without fail, trusting completely in our integrity as commanders.

It would be dastardly indeed to leave them now, facing the enemy in the mud in Cela while we proceeded south to the Republic to possibly bask in the sun on some beach or other while getting ourselves together again for the normal rigours of army life.

We refused to do it.

I even got a signal from the general in command of operations in Angola informing me personally that the Chief of the Army had ordered me to return to South Africa. The Brigadier brought me the signal and I asked him to pretend that he could not locate me. The Brigadier readily agreed.

Toon and his men now also pulled out for the south. They were being replaced by a completely fresh armoured-car squadron.

Again there was a party of somewhat less inhibited nature than the previous one for Corky, the red monster being somewhat basic in his general outlook on life.

They gave me a case of beer as a parting gesture because I was the only commander who had not lost an armoured car in action. A whole case of South African beer was like gold, in view of the scarcity of this particular commodity.

We reminisced somewhat raucously, drank and generally made a nuisance of ourselves to our sleeping neighbours. The presence at the party of some well-known chopper pilots did not help to tone down the noise.

The next morning a bleary-eyed Toon strapped his little 60 mm armoured car to his huge frame and with a laugh and rude comments he signalled his squadron southwards to the Republic.

They left, smoothly as always, and looking very impressive with their antennas whipping in the breeze.

During the Savannah Campaign Toon had only evacuated one of his armoured cars back to South Africa, although he had several shot out by the enemy. The rest he repaired in his own light workshop troop, which theoretically, was supposed to be beyond their capability.

In my mind I could still see them at Catengue, the 90 mm guns cracking away with smoke, flame and fury at FAPLA, and at Benguela where they sat in little knots on the open airfield under rocket, anti-tank and mortar fire, always shooting and always manoeuvring towards the enemy or leading the advance with my infantry and deploying like lightning to return fire the moment we hit a delaying position.

I remember the bearded and laughing faces of the troop leaders while we sat down to a hasty meal of bread, cheese and beer in the officers' mess at Sá da Bandeira.

I also remembered that Toon's squadron never left my infantry in the lurch. They were always up there with them, supporting them in style when required. They were genuinely concerned about my platoons as I was.

In fact, a bond of affection grew up between the armoured cars and my infantry. They considered my troops to be the most professional infantry troops in the whole of Angola, rightly or wrongly. I was flattered all the same.

My troops just loved the armoured cars, especially the big devastating bang it carried in the 90 mm main gun.

All our friends had gone. I had handed over the battalion to Frank for the moment while I tried to get the guerrillas off the ground. It was at this moment that Paul decided to abscond also.

When I got to my "abode", in a rather filthy and rickety little farm cottage, I found no supper or coffee waiting.

Upon enquiries it appeared that Paul had packed his gear and just left without telling anybody where he was going.

The next day I dropped in at Frank's headquarters to find Paul sitting there as large as life. Frank was grinning from ear to ear. "Paul could not take you any longer," he said. "He decided to come and serve as my batman." Frank already had a batman. He now had two, while I suddenly had to do without one.

I suppose I was rather nasty to Paul, especially during the heat of battle when I had the bad habit of getting downright sarcastic. So I left Paul in peace and rather thankfully moved in with the Reccies where the food was much better and the company much more congenial, all of them being old troops of mine.

I never saw Paul again and the need for his interpreting ability had, in any case, fallen away.

While waiting for the "powers that be" to make up their minds regarding my troops' rest and recuperation, we moved around the countryside to look at what were once very productive farm units.

The Portuguese authorities settled Portuguese farmers from the mother country on farms that resembled the Israeli kibbutz system. Small villages with pretty cottages were established with the adjoining lands and fields belonging to the farmers living in the village. The rich pastures made cattle and dairy farming very attractive and some of the biggest cheese factories in Angola were found in the area. During our stay, thousands of abandoned well-bred cattle, especially Herefords, Brahmans, Siementhalers and Friesians roamed the plains, some of them beginning to succumb to tick-born diseases.

Santa Comba was the biggest town in the area, beautifully laid out with wide tree-girded streets, nice houses and a huge church, or cathedral, the last completely in disuse while we were there. There were, in fact, numerous signs that the church had been fouled by MPLA before it was "liberated" by Foxbat.

Around the area were dotted some high hills, some reminiscent of Paarl rock, being basically huge bare granite boulders sticking up out of the fertile plain.

The Portuguese also had a very efficient and a very useful agricultural research station in the area. This too was abandoned with all the work gone to waste.

Near one of the huge granite mountains there was a stud farm with about 20 or so Arab stallions still in the stables and many more grazing in adjacent paddocks. The owner had left for Portugal some time previously, leaving all his possessions to the mercy of fighting factions in Angola.

Shortly after the South African forces retired from the area, the Cubans moved in to strip all the cheese factories, grab the breeding stock among horses and cattle and to tin the rest of the beef that could not be exported live to Cuba.

We and UNITA, of course, had also used some of the abandoned cattle as a source of food but never on such a large scale that whole herds were destroyed. We never so much as touched the breeding stock, especially bulls and stallions, as we had hopes that the Portuguese owners would return to their farms one day.

We still had not found out whether the river at Bridge Fourteen was fordable or not.

Previously, Danny was not given much chance to investigate, so I decided to send Diedies, one of my other platoon leaders, and a patrol to establish themselves at night on top of Top Hat from where the bridge and Catofe could be adequately observed during the day.

The only problem was that Top Hat was occupied by FAPLA, but Diedies, a young corporal from 1 Reconnaissance Command, was, in my opinion, quite capable of carrying out the task.

So he left with a patrol in a roundabout way for Top Hat. He finally established himself and one black troop in an observation post on the northern slope above the bridge, virtually in the middle of FAPLA.

There he stayed for a few days and reported back to Frank at his headquarters. It was not long before he gave us the interesting news that hundreds of FAPLA were in the process of wading shoulder deep across the blown-down bridge towards Top Hat. This meant that the river was fordable and also that Top Hat was to be effectively defended by FAPLA, which would make a future crossing of the river by our forces much more difficult. George and Blackie were already planning their assault on Bridge Fourteen and the Catofe area beyond. The possession of Top Hat was therefore vital to them.

FAPLA had to be stopped from occupying the feature. Diedies was given the task of doing it with the help of the 140 mm guns.

Now he was only a very young corporal at the time who had no experience of directing artillery fire, but this did not seem to bother him unduly.

After a rapid course, over the air, in controlling artillery fire, Diedies calmly set about his task from his OP among the FAPLA already on Top Hat. Soon he brought his ranging shots onto the bridge area. He then gleefully went for "fire for effect", using airburst. The results must have astonished even him, being a man of placid nature.

The crossing troops were caught bunching in the open with no overhead cover whatsoever. Literally hundreds were slaughtered.

FAPLA fell back in disorder, virtually a rout, but unfortunately the nearest of our own troops to the retreating enemy were Diedies and his one rather elderly black troop. A follow-up was out of the question. FAPLA vacated the hill with all their forces, which made George's job that much easier about a week later.

When Diedies finally got back, he only had one desire: to see a 140 mm gun from close quarters. He had never seen one before in his life and was suitably impressed with the sheer size of the monster. He also watched with interest the guns being loaded and fired at some distant target. To him it was sheer magic.

I recommended Diedies for the Honoris Crux and this was duly awarded. For my unit, therefore, Top Hat produced two very well-deserved decorations.

To complete the story about Top Hat and Bridge Fourteen one must briefly look at events a week or two later. George seized the hill during an unresisted night assault. He withstood some very heavy artillery, mortar and rocket fire during the rest of that night while the engineers constructed a bridge out of local materials to cross the river.

By first light the next morning, he opened up with his own artillery on nearby hills, crossed with infantry and armoured cars, and generally created consternation and havoc among FAPLA – who were in fact mostly Cubans.

The South Africans killed hundreds, took Catofe, destroyed and captured lots of equipment but were ordered to stop their advance just when Quibala was within their grasp.

At last George could look back with satisfaction on Bridge Fourteen. His setback at Ebo had been well and truly revenged.

Headquarters informed me, just before George commenced his opening moves to take Bridge Fourteen, that my troops had been granted leave and that we could withdraw southwards to our old stamping grounds around M'pupa, Serpa Pinto and Cuito Cuanavale. Connie and his company came back under my command. I gave up all attempts at fighting a guerrilla war and reassumed command of the unit for our withdrawal.

Some new FNLA troops had moved into the Cela area and they were being armed and equipped with some of our weapons and ammunition. They were also being formed into platoons under the command of the newly arrived platoon leaders from the Infantry School, the ones who were supposed to relieve my old platoon leaders.

We were left with only the minimum of weapons to protect ourselves. Further south, fighting had already broken out between UNITA and FNLA after Chipenda's premature departure for Portugal. We could therefore expect some resistance to our passage from UNITA, especially at roadblocks and in the UNITA-controlled towns.

On 11 December we left the mud and rain of Cela. Out came all the FNLA flags to festoon every truck in red, yellow and white banners as we drove southwards to the South West African border at Katitwi, the same place we had crossed some months before.

The troops were in a happy mood and oblivious of the rain and the danger posed by UNITA.

We gave Nova Lisboa, a very strong UNITA centre, a wide berth and headed for Serpa Pinto, historically an FNLA stronghold. By afternoon the next day we arrived. The first batch of my troops were allowed to go home to Serpa Pinto and the surrounding areas as far away as Cuito Cuanavale.

The driver of the flatbed truck with "NOVEL", the name of a construction firm, painted on its side, approached me to enquire whether it would be in order for him to return to his firm which was in Serpa Pinto. Only then did I discover that he was in fact a civilian who, with his truck, had been pushed into service by FNLA four months before to convey troops to us at M'pupa for training. On his arrival I had commandeered both him and his truck and he accompanied us throughout the campaign. His truck, in fact, was at one stage my main firepower base, mounting eight Vickers machine guns in a row. That he and his truck came through unscathed was a miracle, because so often he had to deploy well up forward to enable the gunners to deliver devastating machine-gun fire on FAPLA delaying positions.

What the firm said to their errant driver when he turned up out of the blue after so many months, I shall never know. It was most unlikely that they would have believed his harrowing and exciting stories of his war adventures as a truck driver for the machine-gun platoon of Bravo Group.

We moved south to get as close to the border as possible before nightfall. Foolishly I raced ahead of the main body, completely on my own in my Land Cruiser, to be stopped by a hostile-looking UNITA roadblock at the bridge over the Okavango River at Caiundo. A UNITA soldier came swaggering up to me with the muzzle of his G3 rifle pointing straight at me.

Just below the embankment other troops were turning out to have a look at the white man in his Land Cruiser stopped by their barrier pole placed right across the road. I was still wearing my FNLA cap badge so that anybody could clearly see where my loyalties lay.

My own troops were perhaps 15 minutes behind me. A lot could happen in 15 minutes. I still could not speak the language and here was a UNITA soldier arrogantly shouting something unintelligible at me in Portuguese.

So I lost my temper, jumped out of the Land Cruiser, wrenched the G3 away from the soldier and threw it down the embankment among the rest of them. I then proceeded to demolish the roadblock, kicking over the 44 gallon drums and hurling the barrier pole at the open-mouthed audience below. The UNITA soldier who had tried to stop me, scrambled down to the safety of his friends. He probably thought that I had gone berserk.

I climbed back into my vehicle and drove off, still fuming and hoping that they would pick a quarrel with my troops following on behind, in which case they would be sorted out very quickly.

We thus left Angola, and the Savannah campaign, more or less as we started, the opening scene being our clash with UNITA at Cuvelai and the closing scene my frenzied kicking apart of a UNITA roadblock at Caiundo.

The remainder of my troops were dropped off at Cuangar and Calais. I promised that I would be back in three weeks to collect them for retraining before we were going back into operations.

I had a drink in the bar at Rundu where I waxed eloquent on the satisfaction of commanding in battle troops which one had the good fortune to train oneself. This is not something that happens too frequently to a serving soldier as wars are not that easy to come by, and I thought it worthwhile to discuss my good fortune in this regard. I was particularly full of praise for the conduct of my black FNLA troops.

I expanded on the beauty of seeing one's guns, armoured

cars and infantry deploying with practised ease against the enemy, knowing that the force had been honed into a fine edge, just as one had been taught to do on our numerous promotion and other courses.

The scruffy, undisciplined FNLA battalion I saw at M'pupa started the campaign with a minimum of training. They were fortunately given the chance to learn their warcraft gradually against an ever-stiffening enemy resistance and until the end they fought with perfection and discipline against an enemy that was always stronger in numbers and in firepower.

The battalion had truly been forged in battle. Later on, this was to be the motto we would adopt for the unit.

Unfortunately, at the bar counter one of my friends, who is a very senior medical officer, took the view that I too suffered from battle fatigue. Evidently, certain love of battle and some recklessness, which he seemed to deduce from my tale, were clear indications that all was not well with me upstairs.

So I quickly left the club, went to my room and started to prepare for my holiday with my family at the sea. I was to depart the very next day. Some medic could clap me into some sort of a rehabilitation centre if I tarried too long.

Epilogue

I returned to Rundu four weeks later, having overstayed in the south, to find messages from my old troops awaiting me from the various designated assembly points. "Where was the Commandant and when are we going to start our retraining?"

With the moral support of the GOC, the unit was reformed and Chiote's people were added. Chiote's battalion had, by now, become refugees at a place called Chitado. We started once again – where else but in M'pupa. This time with about 2000 men which we finally whittled down to 1200. We organised the new battalion into eight rifle companies and a support company.

My problem was instructors and platoon leaders. My mission was to fight against SWAPO who were reappearing on our borders as the last South African troops withdrew over the Angolan border.

So the emphasis changed to counter-insurgency operations, with numerous raids against SWAPO bases during the years that followed Savannah.

The unit went from strength to strength under various commanders. Today, they are universally recognised as the best infantry unit in the South African Army. They have had more kills than all the other units combined.

I left the unit in 1977, but before that miserable moment arrived, I had the fortune to be involved in some very remarkable adventures and escapades with my black troops. It must, however, form the subject matter of another book, which perhaps the present commanding officer will write, as he was involved in most of these adventures as one of my officers at the time.

Once UNITA was firmly established, we could leave Angola to continue against SWAPO, which was our main enemy after all.

32 Battalion became a fully fledged South African unit while I was still in command, something I fought for, because I felt that my men deserved a guaranteed future in the country they were serving with impeccable loyalty and courage.

The old black commandantes all became excellent platoon sergeants, men the young second lieutenants and sergeants from the Infantry School could lean on in times of crisis. To this day, these platoon sergeants are the true professionals of the unit.

Many of them have been killed or wounded in action. Some became too old for further combat but are still with the unit in a training or administrative capacity.

The war cemetery at 32 Battalion tells it all. Hundreds of crosses are planted in rows, of men who fell in battle for their adopted country, among them my favourite "Minonambunga" or Bernardo as he was known to some of us. He was the spitting image of pictures I had seen of Shaka: very tall, athletic and aggressive red-rimmed eyes, a powerful man in battle.

I had lost all my Portuguese platoon leaders in one week, now known as "black week" in 32 Battalion. Danny and Silva were killed on a mine together with four others, one a South African corporal. Robbie, with the afro hairstyle, was killed when a bloody great truck, overtaking in dusty conditions, drove into him straight from the front while he was evacuating the injured from that particular mine incident. A few days before, his younger brother had been killed in an ambush.

Costa, although not serving with me, lost his life on the border some years later. He had married a lovely South African girl.

Of the original South African platoon leaders and company commanders few are still with us today. Connie, Mecchie and Fingers were all killed in action.

Jack, or Red Fox as I called him, was injured in an incident with explosives and is completely blind today. He remains, however, as cheerful and full of life as ever.

Corky became a brigadier and I see him from time to time at formal functions, resplendent in his white tropicals and medals, although not his Novo Redondo medals; a great pity.

Toon became quite tame under the patient tuition of his wife and is now a colonel. One can now, at least, go out on the town with him without getting embarrassed.

Delville stayed on with his Bushmen until 1978, after which they made him a brigade commander in the SWA Territorial Army. I often pass through Windhoek and always take the opportunity to go and chew the fat with him. He should write a book about 31 Battalion.

Frank also eventually became a brigade commander, this time of the Parachute Brigade.

My unit collected quite a number of decorations and medals for our efforts during Savannah. If I remember rightly, we received three Honoris Cruxes, one Southern Cross decoration and two commendation medals. Some applications, unfortunately, were turned down. The Honoris Cruxes went to Connie, Danny and Diedies and they were all well deserved.

Zulu, as a whole, got quite a few decorations and medals as well. Corky got a much deserved Southern Cross decoration, but he should really have received the decoration instead.

Delville's unit got several decorations, also at least two Honoris Cruxes that I am aware of. At least one of Toon's troop leaders got an Honoris Crux.

So the honours duly arrived, but the greatest of them all – the respect, affection and trust my black troops bestowed on me – knocked all honours and glory into a cocked hat.

I had brought my black troops out of Angola when their own leaders had abandoned them. To them this was the most vital and important factor which will tie them to South Africa's interests and future as long as they can draw breath and are capable of fighting.

List of Names

The Brigadier	Brigadier Dawie Schoeman
Corky	Colonel Koos van Heerden
Delville	Commandant Delville Lindford
Toon	Major Toon Slabbert
Frank	Major Frank Bestbier
Phillip	Commandant Phillip du Preez
Coen	Major Coen Upton
Jack	Captain Jack Dippenaar
Connie	Lieutenant Connie van Wyk
Costa	Staff Sergeant Costa Mauráo
Silva	Sergeant Silva Soares
Danny	Sergeant Danny Roxa
Robbie	Sergeant Robbie Ribeiro
Oupa	Corporal Oupa van Dyk
Fingers	Corporal Fingers Kruger
Diedies	Corporal Diederichs
Mecchie	Corporal Mecchie van der Merwe
Nel	Corporal Nel
Anton	Corporal Anton Retief
Smokey	Captain Smokey Bouwer
Schalkie	Colonel Schalkwyk
Blackie	Colonel Blackie Swart
George	Commandant George Kruys
Dries	Major Dries van Coller
Willie	Commandant Wilkie Kotze
Grobbie	Captain Grobbelaar
James	Captain James Hills